In the Midst of It All

In the Midst of It All

Depression and the Bible Verses
that Got Me Through

Jezanie Warjri

RESOURCE *Publications* · Eugene, Oregon

IN THE MIDST OF IT ALL
Depression and the Bible Verses that Got Me Through

Resource Publications
An Imprint of Wipf and Stock Publishers
199 W. 8th Ave., Suite 3
Eugene, OR 97401

www.wipfandstock.com

PAPERBACK ISBN: 978-1-6667-1828-7
HARDCOVER ISBN: 978-1-6667-1829-4
EBOOK ISBN: 978-1-6667-1830-0

09/07/21

To all the tired souls, mental health is worth fighting for.
To all the troubled minds, it's okay to ask for help.
To all the faithless hearts, God is always near.
To all the loved ones, thank you for your support.
To all the strangers, I hope you find what you're looking for.

Even though I walk through the valley of the shadow
of death, I will fear no evil, for you are with me;
your rod and your staff, they comfort me.

—PSALM 23:4, ESV

If only I could tell you
How I'm feeling
Describe to you in words
That would fail
That each passing day
My hope grows bigger
My will mightier than my fears
Nights become cooler
Days more pleasant
And a prayer that one day
I could tell you all.

—JEZANIE WARJRI

Contents

Introduction

DEPRESSION AND ANXIETY MADE me believe I wasn't a good Christian. If worry is the opposite of faith, mine was feeling tainted beyond grace. I don't recall my first experience with depression, but I do remember the feeling vividly.

I grew up in a healthy environment and a stable family. My family is a wholesome Christian family. Nurtured on Christian values and principles of faith, prayer, love, respect, and so on, I was quite familiar with Christian norms.

As far as family dynamics go, there were the frequent family arguments, disagreements, and scolding. Growing up, my parents prohibited us from drinking and listening to secular music. This made no sense to me. Music and alcohol does affect your mood and senses, but secular music or responsible drinking does not necessarily account for the most abominable behavior. Aside from these rules I found confining, my upbringing was rather normal.

So why was I always fearful?

On random nights my stomach would clench, my chest would tighten, my heart rate would intensify, my mind would drift off to endless, meaningless thoughts, my teeth would some-time grind, and unexpectedly, an overwhelming feeling of fear and emptiness took over. There were frequent times I would go to sleep only to be woken up by hallucinations and terror caused by sleep paralysis.

For those who have never experienced depression or anxiety, I envy you. I don't wish such an experience upon anyone. But for some like me who have gone through cycles of depression and anxiety every year and every season, life takes a turn.

Depression made me feel worthless. Depression made me paranoid. Depression made me go through sleepless nights. Depression made it difficult to concentrate. Depression made me question my beliefs. Depression made it difficult to form healthy relationships. Depression made me have anxious and delusional thoughts.

Depression: a lonesome, turmoil-filled road.

It's difficult to narrate such a personal experience. Even more difficult to make others understand. I don't expect someone to comprehend even a fraction of it, but someone's display of genuine support can turn this state of lonely restlessness into one of savored solitude.

Let's call these bouts of depression "episodes." The only thing that has been able to offer any sort of comfort and assurance during my many episodes are biblical promises.

My episodes would make me loathe social interactions. I would curl up in a blanket, tuck myself into bed, and hope not a soul would peer at me. My only source of comfort would keep me company.

Mental health has longed been regarded as a challenging topic in churches and Christian circles. In the small town in India where I grew up, mental health is not only kicked to the bottom of topics talked about, it is seen as a sign of emotional and spiritual weakness. Churches in Northeast India are not too forthcoming about discussing mental health. Rarely do I hear of church leaders expressing concern for the growing number of mental health problems among church members, particularly younger people. Depression and anxiety are common, and churches need to address this more and break the stigma by welcoming sermons and small-group ministries. Churches need to foster a culture of acceptance, compassion, and empathy toward people struggling with chronic mental illness.

I've been told my struggle is a sickness from Satan himself. I have cringed and shuddered, but most of all, I've felt hopelessness. There's nothing more discouraging than an unkind word.

On my most difficult days, I'd flip through pages, browse journals and blogs, and spend helpless hours looking for answers.

"Consult a therapist."

"Cultivate healthy habits."

"De-stress."

"Confide in someone."

I did it all, and nothing helped.

Soon, I gave up. I gave in. Uneducated and unaware, I began my spiral journey downward.

Insomnia.

Poor concentration.

Unwanted/intrusive/delusional thoughts.

Uncontrolled emotional outbursts.

Fatigue.

These were some of the effects and symptoms of untreated depression and anxiety.

Throughout my mid- and late twenties, I struggled for an identity. I struggled with relationships and forming lasting connections. I struggled with self-confidence and doing what I really wanted to do. I struggled with depression and anxiety and understanding their effect on my health. I spent my time desperately searching for purpose. Wandering through my days—trying to get through another day—was a short, celebrated achievement. I spent restless days hoping it would get better, but it never did. For years I have cried out to God to make me *whole*. I didn't know what *whole* meant, but there was a void in my heart and chaos in my head, and I desperately needed for all of it to stop. Many times, *whole* looked like a successful, fulfilling career, a loving partner, a comfortable life, or a house I could call my own. I couldn't understand why I so desperately needed to feel complete.

There is no story of a blissful light at the end of the tunnel. This is one of an ordinary life lived by simply making the most of what is given. I *can* say I feel more confident with myself, more stable with my emotions, and more hopeful for my future. What made me get here? Letting go of extreme, zealous ambitions by focusing on my present and pursuing what is meant for me. What helped me find acceptance and comfort? Bible verses:

Then Jesus said, "Come to me, all of you who are weary
and carry heavy burdens, and I will give you rest."
Matt 11:28, NIV

He has removed our sins as far from
us as the east is from the west.
Ps 103:12, NIV

Keep your lives free from the love of money
and be content with what you
have, because God has said,
"Never will I leave you;
never will I forsake you."
Heb 13:5, NIV

"I will not cause pain without allowing some-
thing new to be born," says the LORD.
Isa 66:9, NCV

I praise you because I am fearfully and wonderfully
made; your works are wonderful, I know that full well.
Ps 139:14, NIV

But the fruit of the Spirit is love, joy, peace, forbear-
ance, kindness, goodness, faithfulness, gentleness and
self-control. Against such things there is no law.
Gal 5:22–23, NIV

Bible verses helped me get through the harshest of nights. I spent a lot of time researching medical explanations and secular guidance on every aspect of my life. Though some proved helpful and informative, they were not successful. I needed more than practical tips, statistical how-tos, and scientific approaches. It wasn't theological reasoning that I was searching for. I needed comfort on distressing nights, assurances for my agonizing thoughts, solutions to my inexplainable problems, and guidance for purposeful living.

Introduction

One desperate Sunday morning, I decided to keep at heart a few verses that quenched my distraught heart. For months afterward, I disciplined myself to never google a word when my hopeless search for answers got the best of me. Instead, I googled Bible verses.

Every time my anxiety crept up on me or depression left me feeling hopeless, I googled a Bible verse. For every feeling or decision I had to make, I had a Bible verse to refer back to.

Afraid that my future was looking meaningless, I held on to Jer 29:11:

> "For I know the plans I have for you," declares the LORD, "plans to prosper you and not to harm you, plans to give you hope and a future." (NIV)

When I woke up in the middle of the night filled with terror and anxiety, I would read and meditate on 2 Tim 1:7:

> For God has not given us a spirit of fear and timidity, but of power, love, and self-discipline. (NLT)

On days when I questioned myself and felt unworthy, I held on to Luke 12:24:

> Look at the ravens. They don't plant or harvest or store food in barns, for God feeds them. And you are far more valuable to him than any birds! (NLT)

When God felt distant and nowhere to be found, I trusted what was written in Isa 41:10:

> So do not fear, for I am with you; do not be dismayed, for I am your God. I will strengthen you and help you; I will uphold you with my righteous right hand. (NIV)

Whenever I felt down and blue, the Psalms lifted my spirit, such as Ps 42:11:

> Why, my soul, are you downcast? Why so disturbed within me? Put your hope in God, for I will yet praise him, my Savior and my God. (NIV)

This may sound extreme to some and ridiculous to others. For me, it added perspective and shaped how I think about matters that are beyond simply my belief in God. My views and feelings on personal suffering started changing. It soon became pain I was yet to overcome. It wasn't that I was unaware of Bible verses and principles of Christian faith prior to this, but this was a conscious effort to not only trust the Scriptures but also to believe they have unforeseen answers waiting for me.

The word *depression* is not found in the Bible, but it is referred to by other terms, such as 'downcast', 'troubled' and 'brokenhearted.' The Psalms are filled with praises from a troubled heart. David writes songs of praises to God in the midst of his misery. He cries out to God, looking for comfort.

"The Lord is near to the brokenhearted and saves those who are crushed in Spirit" (Ps 34:18 ESV).

I made a promise to myself: no matter what may come, I will always choose God. I decided to write down my feelings. This became a ritual and a habit that started sowing seeds in my new way of life. The answers I desperately looked for turned pale, irrelevant, and insignificant. My anxious thoughts hovered above me like dark clouds before a storm, but like rain on the driest of places, the promises in Scripture provided comfort, assurance, and renewal, inspiring me to pour out words of praise and gratitude.

Grace

Amazing grace
I once was lost, but now I'm found
Was blind, but now I see
'Twas grace that taught my heart to fear
And grace my fears relieved
This grace I once heard about
But fear made me believe it wasn't for me.
This precious grace is now all I know of
It guided me through wildernesses
Trampled on all my fears and anxieties
This grace has sufficed me through loneliness
Became everything I couldn't be
It took despair and hopelessness
And cursed them to the ground.
This grace taught me strength
Showed me comfort, became my friend
It revealed unto me
What my thoughts had hidden away
I was blind, but now I see!

Part 1

Understanding Anxiety and Depression

*For the LORD grants wisdom! From his mouth
come knowledge and understanding.*

PROVERBS 2:6, NLT

DEPRESSION CAN BLUR REALITY and distort what really is. It can make the future seem hopeless and undesirable. While you used to be excited about weekends and café meetups with friends, now the thought of any of it only makes you feel worn out and uninterested. You want to stay in, but being alone makes the inside of your chest sink into loneliness. You want to carefully construct words that can justify why you have been missing from all your friends' social gatherings. If only they understood what you're feeling and what you've been through—it would make things easier for you. But what you're feeling is something no one can understand. There is nothing anyone can say or do to make it all better. Your words may fail and come short, and they'll only reveal the insignificance of it all. Sometimes, you pick yourself up and try your best to go about your day, and for days—even weeks—you feel like yourself again. Making plans for the future and looking forward to the party your coworkers are all hyped up for? That doesn't seem so bad. And then out of nowhere, it all doesn't matter anymore. Everything and everyone around you cannot fill the emptiness that is so apparent. The nights are getting difficult. Falling asleep without random thoughts bombarding you is almost impossible. You only wish the day would go by without you getting out of bed or making any effort whatsoever.

You may not realize it, but soon the things that once brought you joy and calmness only exasperate you. The smallest of things make you break down and lose control over your emotions. Expectations and plans for the future become dark and bleak. Suddenly, everything isn't the way it's supposed to be. Let's not even talk about the future. You don't want to die. You are not suicidal. You just need all of this to end!

Depression isn't just in the head. It isn't just for the weaker souls. Depression can hit you out of nowhere without clear reasons and make you feel like an undeserving victim. Being mentally and emotionally healthy isn't a blessing for the good at heart and boundless in faith. Every person on earth has a right to a healthy mind and body, but that isn't the case. Unfortunately, there are people everywhere fighting a battle of their own, and I am one of them.

I had a difficult time accepting the fact that I had depression. Before I was diagnosed and put on medication, I had all kinds of explanations, excuses, and justifications that only made sense to me. I tried to educate myself and be rational and fair to my well-being, but I was in denial. And the biggest reason was my misconception about depression. I don't know if it was self-educated or if I was conditioned by external factors, but I thought depression was characterized by one emotion: sadness. And I wasn't sad.

I confided in a few people close to me, telling them I was anxious—that it must have been anxiety and that it was causing me some problems. I thought the unmanageable thoughts in my head could only be an outcome of anxiety. The sleepless, tiresome nights weren't normal. I thought, it must be stress. But all of it isn't something to get all worked up about. This is what I told myself every time anxiety and depression got me.

Maybe that is what depression does. It keeps you in the dark, isolated and far from feeling good. It makes you feel undeserving without reason. It makes you believe in the worse. If it's bad, it must be true. Depression constitutes an illness because it is nothing but an illness. It isn't because of you, who you are as a person, or what you deserve. It's a mental state that causes symptoms and illness and deprives you of normalcy.

Many books on depression and anxiety disorders have been published throughout the years that have given readers insight and offered methods of treatments and coping strategies. Many of them are helpful and informative. This book isn't one of them. This book is a personal account of dealing with depression and anxiety and the calm I experience every time I read assuring verses from the Bible.

Right now you may protest, "I've done that! I've attended church and listened to all kinds of sermons and read all kinds of books, but I'm still depressed!"

This book isn't a testimony of overcoming depression through relentless faith, prayer, and reading. It isn't one about how my Christian faith got me out of it. This isn't about religion. This is about comfort, peace, assurance, hope, and so much more. This is about God's presence in the midst of the chaos.

Since depression and anxiety are biological disorders caused by chemical imbalances, mood regulations by the brain, stressful life events, medical problems, and many other factors that are beyond our control, it's important for people to understand what depression and anxiety—or any other mental illness—really are and how they affect people. Since depression affects the mind more than the body, our mind become susceptible to changes and disorder. It causes chaos and vulnerability and affects our moods, thoughts, and even decisions.

This book explores certain emotional ranges and thoughts that are most commonly caused by depression and anxiety. Most of them are drawn from my own personal struggles. I am not a doctor or an expert on mental health. Therefore, I've included this chapter containing citations from eminent authors about the psychological aspect of mental illness. This is to help readers understand the effects of depression and anxiety on our mental health and everyday life.

In these chapters, you will also read about how certain feelings and emotions are misinterpreted and mishandled, and how symptoms of depression and anxiety can play a huge role in distorting certain views and personal beliefs.

Many are fighting their own battle with anxiety and depression. I am one of them. I am not on the other end. I am still on the road to recovery and healthy living. This is an honest account about how long-term depression and anxiety affected my faith and mental health, and how I found the strength and comfort from Bible verses to fight through it all.

Spiritual coping strategies, cognitive therapy, and mindfulness approaches have long been advised by authors and psychology experts. Most cognitive therapy involves identifying certain thoughts, ideologies, and beliefs that contribute to depression and anxiety and replacing them with positive, realistic, and productive thoughts.

The Bible contains verses for countering fear, insights for a sound mind, calls to healthy thinking, assurances for troubling times, hopeful messages for periods of uncertainty, promises of healing, reminders to lay the past where it belongs, and so much more.

Disruption techniques are also considered by secular studies to help cope with anxiety, such as talking to family and friends, taking up a hobby, or any healthy activity that helps disrupt or distract the worry. Reading is one technique that reinforces positive distraction. Bible verses that offer assurance and solace can be helpful during distressing and faithless times.

Adopting healthy practices is principal for a sound mind and healthy body. One of the practices that helped me the most to power through anxiety was light reading and calm, reassuring music. Typically, these were Bible verses and contemporary worship songs. A few healthy practices to help manage depression and anxiety are mentioned in the later part of the book.

In his book *Cognitive Behavioral Therapy*, Lawrence Wallace writes:

Part 1: Understanding Anxiety and Depression

Anxiety is a normal emotion, but it can get out of control. It helps us in physically dangerous situations by activating a part of the automatic nervous system and preparing the body for fighting or running away. The automatic nervous system controls all our involuntary activities, like breathing, heartbeat, and digestion. It has two components, the sympathetic and the parasympathetic nervous systems. The sympathetic nervous system can be thought of as a gas pedal. It triggers the fight-or-flight response, resulting in faster breathing and heart rate, the release of adrenaline and other stress hormones, and a spike in blood glucose levels. . . . Worse, it stays activated when stress levels stay high, causing actual physical damage to our bodies including inflammation, high blood pressure, and a higher risk of heart disease. It also leads to symptoms that make day-to-day life more difficult and less enjoyable including insomnia, a sense of dread, irritability, restlessness, poor concentration, sweating, and feeling on edge.

The good thing is that we can stop this physiological cascade of stress responses by doing things that activate the parasympathetic nervous system. The parasympathetic nervous system is like the brake pedal. It is activated when the brain receives messages that it is safe to relax, resulting in slower heart rate and breathing, a drop in stress-hormone levels, and improved digestion. Many things increase parasympathetic nervous system activity, including deep breathing, mantra meditation, yoga, repetitive prayer, tai chi, being in nature, visualizing calm scenes, and being with supportive friends or loved ones.[1]

Anxiety disorders are distinguished from everyday, normal anxiety in that they involve anxiety that is more intense (for example, panic attacks), that lasts longer (anxiety that may persist for months or longer instead of going away after a stressful situation has passed), or that leads to phobias that interfere with your life. There are many factors that contribute to anxiety disorders. The most common cause is cumulative stress acting over time. There are also several other causes that predispose people to anxiety, such

1. Wallace, *Cognitive Behavioral Therapy*, x.

as heredity, childhood circumstances, and biological causes. Anxiety disorder can also be short-term, triggered by stress and trauma. The last factor is maintaining habits such as engaging in anxious self-talk, holding mistaken beliefs, having a high-stress lifestyle, and listening to feelings of meaninglessness and purposelessness.

Most anxiety disorders are treatable and get better with therapy, medications, and healthy living. Common types of disorders are social-anxiety disorder, panic disorder, generalized anxiety disorder, phobias, obsessive-compulsive disorder, post-traumatic stress disorder, and anxiety caused by medical conditions and substance abuse.

Depression is more than just a state of feeling "sad" or "down." I never used to think I had depression because I had this notion in my head that depression is only characterized by feelings of sadness, hopelessness, or worthlessness regarding myself, my past and future, and/or my circumstances. This was not always how I felt. My understanding of depression was highly flawed. Depression can manifest itself in many ways. There were nights when I felt all kinds of emotions, only to wake up the next day feeling "emotionally numb." I knew I was anxious, but I didn't understand the lack of concentration and the uncontrolled and unwanted thoughts that ran through my mind for days. For lack of better words, it felt like there was an audio-visual device stuck inside my head and it wouldn't turn off. It drained my focus and attention and left me emotionally and physically exhausted. Unaware, I believed there was something not right with me.

In her book *This is Depression*, Diane McIntosh gives this definition of depression:

> Depression . . . [is] a highly personal experience. It doesn't just cause miserable emotional and physical symptoms: it also interferes with an individual's ability to function, whether at work, school, home, or in social situations. When you're depressed, just getting out of bed can feel overwhelmingly difficult, so it's little wonder that performing at work, completing school tasks, parenting effectively, or caring for yourself and your family can be difficult or even impossible. Furthermore, depression is

a barrier to socializing with friends and participating in previously enjoyed recreational activities, like exercise, hobbies, or going to the movies.[2] . . . Most people suffering from depression will experience some degree of anxiety, which usually means they are worrying excessively about everyday things (e.g., health, work, finances). Additionally, anxiety may include constantly feeling like something terrible is about to happen, ruminating about negative thoughts, feeling a loss of control, difficulty concentrating because of focusing on worries, or feeling restless, tense, keyed up, or on edge—all without a clear cause.[3]

Depression can have symptoms beyond being in a depressed mood on most days or nearly everyday. Other symptoms include a diminished interest or pleasure in daily activities, weight loss or weight gain, a decrease or increase in appetite, insomnia or sleeping too much, restlessness or feeling slowed down, fatigue or loss of energy, feelings of worthlessness and guilt, inability to concentrate, and/or recurring thoughts of death, suicide, and self-harm.

Other common disorders are panic or anxiety attacks and intrusive thoughts. A panic attack is a sudden, intense fear or anxiety that may cause you to have shortness of breath or dizziness. You may feel out of control, and your heart may pound. What you need to keep in mind is that after every panic or anxiety attack, it is normal to feel tense and fearful. Fear often causes your brain to produce many unwanted thoughts that feel odd and confusing. These intrusive thoughts are common and are symptoms of anxiety disorders, obsessive-compulsive disorder (OCD), and post-traumatic stress disorder. When dealing with intrusive thoughts, it is best to dismiss them as meaningless. They are just thoughts that are not a reflection of your character or your beliefs.

Another common symptom is ruminating over thoughts of past events and replaying scenarios, conversations, and problems over and over again. During my episodes of depression and anxiety, I would either sit or lie in bed ruminating for hours and hours over

2. McIntosh, *This Is Depression*, 5.

3. McIntosh, *This Is Depression*, 11.

past scenarios that may or may not have happened. Depression would paint these scenarios negatively. This habit robbed me of my sleep and peace of mind and fueled feelings of fear and sadness that later left me feeling emotionally drained or numb. I would obsess over these thoughts for days to the point of exhaustion.

Rumination is common and can happen to anyone with depression. Rumination can cause a person to fixate on past events and issues that concern him or her, trying to make sense of them or imagining different outcomes for them.

Anxiety and depression are manageable and treatable. We can practice managing them by adopting certain methods that can calm our nervous system. Proper medications help too. Through the years, I have slowly learnt to practice control and to calm my anxious thoughts that can slowly wreak havoc on my emotions if allowed to go astray. When feeling depressed or anxious, I remind myself that the feeling is only temporary. Whatever fear and feelings of despair are only a result of my nervous system reacting to the release of stress hormones. I give myself a few minutes to calm down, exercise deep breathing, and reason with my thoughts, and when the panic subsides, I turn on some light gospel songs, read some assuring Bible verses, and take a walk!

Part 2

Biblical Knowledge

Man shall not live by bread alone, but by every
word that comes from the mouth of God.

MATTHEW 4:4, NIV

THERE IS NO SCHEDULE or formula to know God. The Bible is not an instruction manual on how to become a better person or a better Christian. The Bible is an account of the truth.

Throughout the Bible, you'll see passages of God saying, "If my people listen to my word and obey my commands." God makes specific reference to who he is talking to. We are his children, and the word of God applies to us. If we choose to listen to his voice and obey him, good things will follow according to his promises.

Once, someone close said to me, "I don't believe in God! Where is he? Who said we can hear him?"

We may not hear a loud, thundering voice from the heavens, but we can all hear God's voice as conviction in our hearts. The choice to listen to that conviction is solely up to us.

Yes, certain great people of faith—like Moses, Abraham, and many other biblical characters—have had great encounters with God. Moses had a one-on-one interaction with God on Mount

Sinai. If you start comparing your life with the ones from the Bible, you may end up feeling left behind. Bible stories are life examples. We choose to walk with God in the same way biblical men and women did. Their lives are meant to teach and inspire us. God wants us to thrive, to lead, to teach, to pray, and to have good role models.

Our lives may fail in comparison with the lives of many people in the Bible, but it doesn't have to take a great encounter to have great faith. It takes a mustard seed of faith to believe, and it takes a simple act of obedience to have a great relationship with God. We need to take more responsibility for our relationship with God. Well, I need to. I admit—I have been one of those people who have faith in God but who blame him when things don't work out. And I am also one of those people who think and pray before doing anything, and then I start questioning if God even cares about my prayers. I know very well he exists, but is he present in my life? I don't know—sometimes it doesn't feel that way.

How can God come through for me when I block him out with doubts and disbelief? If I could explain to you in words what my faith used to be, I'd start by saying I was a girl who believed wholeheartedly, but things didn't always go the right way for her. This made her question, but it also made her search in depth for truth, knowledge, and understanding. I found that the bridge keeping the distance between me and God—and me and my mental health—was created by me alone.

I had to ask myself very difficult questions:

Am I walking away from God yet expecting great things from him?

I do love him, but I struggle to trust him?

Do I believe in his commandments but follow through with my own decisions?

Am I a professed Christian but lack faith?

If one or all of these questions apply to you as well, then I am in good company. I was raised Christian all of my life and I go to church on every Sunday, but I struggle with my faith every day. One of the things I've struggled with the most is finding my worth in God. In my teens, I was very much familiar with the phrase "your identity is in Christ," but I didn't know what it meant or how much truth it held.

Who can say that they are perfect and untainted in faith and belief? Even the most righteous grapple with faith, knowing or unknowingly, but those who seek God with all their hearts will find him. "Seek the LORD your God, you will find him if you seek him with all your heart and with all your soul." (Deut 4:29 NIV).

This is something I've been trying to do: seek him with all my heart—not seeking some version of God in my head or the expectations of what should happen when I find him, but simply seeking him because he is God.

Knowing the Bible does not mean you need the ability to paraphrase it word by word. It does not mean you need the disciplinary knowledge of biblical scholars. I still have problems finding verses in the Bible because I can't remember which chapter and verse number it's from. Knowing the Bible means knowing the heart and character of God and what can be resurrected through your faith. It means you know what has been graciously handed to you, and where and how you can use this to advantage in your life.

The Bible isn't difficult to read and understand. It is not written in technical, philosophical language that makes it difficult for some to interpret. The central message of Scripture is rather clear for all to understand, but there are certain passages that require a little effort in discerning the meaning and what it means in relationship to our Christian faith and beliefs.

In the words of R. C. Sproul:

> There are some sections that are profoundly difficult to understand, and it can be helpful to learn how to recognize certain forms and patterns in Scripture that enable us to more easily discern the point of the text. The Bible is not just a storybook. It contains historical narrative, poetry, parables, letters, and highly imaginative symbolic literature (called apocalyptic literature, such as the book of Revelation or the book of Daniel). These different

styles, or forms, of Scripture require certain basic rules of interpretation in order to understand them correctly.[1]

Knowing God requires learning. Learning the things of God is the beginning of wisdom. Get to know God and his word. The Bible is God-breathed. It is very important to know what his words are. The answer to every problem or heartache is all written in the Bible. When you know the word of God intimately, you can stand firm in your faith. When the world seems to be against you and everything you've believed is tested, the Bible says you have armor that's mightier than what is against you.

"Take the helmet of salvation, and the sword of the Spirit, which is the word of God" (Eph 6:17 NIV).

Bible Verses to Remember

For no word from God will ever fail.
Luke 1:37, NIV

But he said, "Blessed rather are those who
hear the word of God and keep it!"
Luke 11:28, ESV

For the word of God is alive and powerful. It is
sharper than the sharpest two-edged sword, cutting
between soul and spirit, between joint and marrow.
It exposes our innermost thoughts and desires.
Heb 4:12, NLT

All Scripture is inspired by God and is useful to teach
us what is true and to make us realize what is wrong
in our lives. It corrects us when we are wrong and
teaches us to do what is right. God uses it to prepare
and equip his people to do every good work.
2 Tim 3:16–17, NLT

---

1. Sproul, *What Is Biblical Wisdom?*, 14.

Part 2: Biblical Knowledge

*Heaven and earth will pass away, but
my words will not pass away.*
Matt 24:35, NIV

*The grass withers, the flower fades, but the
word of our God will stand forever.*
Isa 40:8, NLT

Lies vs. Truth

God is not man, that he should lie, or a son of
man, that he should change his mind.

NUMBERS 23:19, ESV

WHAT HAPPENED IN THE Garden of Eden?

In short, Satan spoke to Eve and deceived her into disobeying God.

Most of us are familiar with this story, but how many of us understand that Satan still uses the same old tactic of deceiving people that leads us to believe lies and disobey God? And for some, it leads to sin and spiritual alienation from God.

The Bible says, "The serpent said to the woman, 'Did God actually say, "You shall not eat of any tree in the garden"?'" (Gen 3:1 ESV).

Satan in the form of a serpent said this to Eve, deceiving her about God's intentions.

The truth was that God allowed Adam and Eve to eat from all the trees except one. And then Satan further lied by saying, "For God knows that when you eat of it your eyes will be opened, and you will be like God, knowing good and evil" (Gen 3:5 ESV).

But what happened was this: "Then the eyes of both were opened, and they knew that they were naked" (Gen 3:7 ESV).

Nothing Satan said was close to the truth.

John 8:44 says that "Satan was a murderer from the beginning, and does not stand in the truth, because there is no truth in him. When he lies, he speaks out of his own character, for he is a liar and the father of lies" (ESV).

There may not be a physical tree of the knowledge of good and evil in our lives, but in what way is Satan deceiving you?

"Am I enough?"

"Am I deserving of love?"

"Am I my past?"

"Am I qualified enough for the job?"

"God's good to everyone except me!"

In the same way that Satan deceived Eve, he can deceive us. Satan can distort the truth, like he did with Eve. He can form lies and half-truths in our heads. You need to stand firm in your belief in order to discern between what God said and what was conceived through lies and deceit.

Another mediator of lies is people. When people lie to us, especially at an early age or at a time when we are most vulnerable, their lies distort the truth of our own lives over time. We begin to believe and live by the lie. This can shape people's behavior and thinking, and it can cause behavioral and emotional problems.

If you have been lied to or have believed a lie, that may have caused anxiety, depression, stress, or bipolar or eating disorders, and it may have caused you to resort to substance abuse or irrational emotional and/or physical outbursts at the people least deserving of it. You may have had suicidal thoughts and ideation or thoughts of self-harm and self-loathing. You may have blown a career or job opportunity once or too many times, and you may have burnt bridges with people you care the most about. Whatever may have happened throughout your life, remind yourself to never let a lie be the reason that holds you back from redeeming yourself and achieving a stable, self-fulfilling life. Mend those broken relationships, build that career, and manage your emotional and mental health. A lie is just words that can be countered by the truth.

We can learn the power of truth from the life of Jesus himself on earth. During his early life, Jesus was driven by the Holy Spirit into the wilderness for the purpose of being put to the test. Jesus fasted forty days and forty nights in the wilderness. As the Son of Man, Jesus was hungry and Satan saw his opportunity. Matthew 4:3 tells us that "the tempter came to him and said, 'If you are the Son of God, tell these stones to become bread'" (NIV).

Jesus's response to Satan is evidence of the confidence we should have in the Bible and an example of how we can use it against temptation or any attack from Satan. Quoting from Deut 8:3, Jesus answered, "It is written: 'Man shall not live on bread alone, but on every word that comes from the mouth of God'" (Matt 4:4 NIV).

Like any human being, Jesus was tempted in the same manner as we all are. Satan can manipulate words, twist them around, and use them against us just to drive us away from God. Jesus could have worked a miracle for himself. Instead, he chose to trust his heavenly Father to care for him.

How many of us have believed the lie that if we are God's children, our lives should compare to some imaginative concept of prosperity, wealth, richness, blissful happiness, and every opportunity the world can offer? We may have believed a lie about our significant others, friends, or family, that they don't care for us or don't love us as much as they should. Satan will try to build up barriers between us and those we love using lies and deceit. This doesn't happen only to you and me or only a few of us—it happens to everyone, even the best of us.

Anxiety, depression, and other mental disorders can cause someone to have obsessive thoughts. These are unwanted, intrusive thoughts and can cause great distress in someone. Intrusive thoughts are thoughts that are unwanted and upsetting in nature. They are unpredictable and difficult to control, and can happen at any time. Because of the nature of such thoughts, they can cause feelings of doubt, shame, guilt, confusion, worthlessness, hopelessness, fear, and anxiety. They can be unwanted thoughts of sex, violence, worries, childhood memories, religion and faith, and relationships. It is vital to understand that having such a thought does not mean you actually feel or want to act on it.

Lies vs. Truth

One of the most important things to understand about intrusive thoughts is that they are not true—in fact, quite the opposite. These thoughts are usually the root of our fears. I have an irrational fear about nonconsensual sexual contact, and I had intrusive thoughts that would take control over my mind about sex or sexual acts that are considered immoral. These thoughts would confuse and disgust me, and for a short period of time I would become obsessive over controlling them.

I prayed and meditated, and at times I would read or write to distract myself from these thoughts. Often times these practices helped, and they are encouraged, but you need to remember that when bombarded with intrusive thoughts, your first defense is to dismiss these thoughts. After you've collected yourself and your mind is calm, resort to mindfulness approaches.

Another dysfunctional disorder that leads to anxiety is having beliefs that are assumptions and are formed by what ifs and "if-then," "I should," or "I must" statements. For example: "What if I have a panic attack during the speech?" or "If I made more money, then people would love me more" or "I should make more money so people will love me." These assumptions often come from our desire to find acceptance and to have control.

Assumptions and intrusive thoughts are all examples of lies people believe. They are mere thoughts formed in your mind when triggered by stress and are heightened by unrealistic standards.

You can't go against Satan with tangible weapons. You can't say to him, "I'm going to be so successful; you can't touch me ever." Well, he can. Satan doesn't care if you're rich or poor, sick or well. He'll go after anyone. So what do you do when your godly beliefs are attacked? Use the word of God; it's your spiritual armor (Eph 6:10).

Bible Verses to Remember

*Satan was a murderer from the beginning, not
holding to the truth, for there is no truth in
him. When he lies, he speaks his native language, for he is a liar and the father of lies.*
John 8:44, NIV

*The thief comes only to steal and kill and destroy; I have
come that they may have life, and have it to the full.*
John 10:10, NIV

*Submit yourselves, then, to God. Resist
the devil, and he will flee from you.*
Jas 4:7, NIV

*Be alert and of sober mind. Your enemy the devil prowls
around like a roaring lion looking for someone to
devour. Resist him, standing firm in the faith, because
you know that the family of believers throughout the
world is undergoing the same kind of sufferings.*
1 Pet 5:8–9, NIV

The Greatest Commandment

"You shall love the Lord your God with all your heart and with all your soul and with all your mind. This is the great and first commandment. And a second is like it: You shall love your neighbor as yourself.

MATTHEW 22:37-39, ESV

ONE OF THE MOST sought teachings is the understanding of the meaning of life. People look for pleasures, traits, experiences, and theoretical knowledge to try to understand what gives life meaning. Some may argue it is fame and money and some happiness, but for most people, it is love.

In a modern world, love has been narrowed down to romantic love. The obsession over finding love that ignites sparks and drives you crazy. The kind that blurs your rationality, heightens your most inner desires, and makes you fall into a blissful longing forever and ever.

The ancient Greeks have different names for each type of love. According to them, love is a wide spectrum of emotions including and also extending beyond close, intimate relationships. They are:

- Agape—*Agape* is universal or unconditional love, the love we freely feel for people, things, nature, and God.

- Eros—Named after the Greek god of love, lust, and sex, *eros* is sexual or passionate love, akin to romantic love.

- Philia—Also known as friendship, *philia* is the love that lovers have for each other. It is a *philia* born out of *eros* that in turn feeds back into *eros* to strengthen and develop it.

- Storge—*Storge*, or familiar love, is the kind of love parents have for their children, or that friends and other family members have for each other.

- Ludus—*Ludus* is playful or uncommitted love.

- Mania—*Mania*, or obsessive love, is when a partner is possessive or jealous.

- Pragma—*Pragma* is the kind of love that endures or lasts over time; it is found, for example, between long-established couples.

- Philautia—Finally, *philautia* is self-love. However, there is healthy love akin to self-esteem and an unhealthy love akin to narcissism and self-obsession.[1]

No matter the difference in nature, we all seek love. More importantly, we all seek love that fulfills us. However passive you may feel towards love, we all crave for it. We cannot deny our emotional and physical need for love. As the Greeks have put it, we all long for love that is different in nature.

Notable minds from different centuries and decades have all offered different accounts of the pursuit of love and life. Yet these peculiar and sometimes contradicting accounts only prove that the meaning of love and life is rather mercurial, or ever-changing.

This hasn't changed much in the twenty-first century. The most popular and talked-about topic is love. Philosophers, poets, writers, musicians, and artists have all gained from, contributed to, and monetized the concept of love. Readers, viewers, listeners, and consumers have given in to all intellectual and spiritual solutions and remedies for love-related problems. Despite our best efforts, love can still elude us.

Love can be difficult to understand and difficult to attain. Some say falling in love is easy but staying in love is difficult. Some

1. Liang, "8 Types of Love."

say the easiest part of life is finding someone to love but the most difficult is finding the right person who will love you back. Some say love finds you at the right moment and some say love requires an extensive search of oneself.

People with depression, anxiety, and other chronic illnesses have all gone through times when they feel unloved or undeserving of love. This feeling can last for a while, depending on the emotional status of someone. This doesn't say that people with chronic mental illness, especially those with depression, are incapable of love. Just that there are times when the person is overwhelmed with despair and hopelessness, and these feelings can bring them down. Depression can make a person feel isolated and alone, and this can make a person blame themselves or their loved ones for their pain and affliction. Popular self-help advice will recommend that self-love and self-acceptance are key to emotional growth and relational well-being, but the Bible will tell you otherwise. The foundation for Christ-like love is love for God and love for other people.

There is nothing wrong with taking care of yourself or prioritizing yourself and your needs before anything else. When it's your mental health that's taking a toll, any rational person will advise you to take care of yourself, and you rightfully should. An honest account of my personal experience with depression is that there have been too many times when I secluded myself from people because at the time it was something I needed and wanted. I thought I was doing myself a good deed. Depression left me feeling exhausted from doing nothing. I hated going out. I hated socializing. I hated making plans. All I wanted to do was to stay home. Thankfully, my mother pushed me to be productive, even though I loathed every second of it then—but now I wouldn't have it any other way. I wanted to feel better, and I thought giving in to what felt right would be the right thing to do.

Depression has a harmful way of pulling people into social isolation. Social withdrawal or isolation only worsens depression. Anxiety can do the same thing. What we need to remember when depression is making it difficult to get up from bed is that what you're feeling is only a result of depression. You have control over your depression, not the other way around. Some degree of withdrawal from a depressed episode is normal. People staying in for a day without any social interaction because of depression and going about their daily life the next day or two to three days later is not a cause for concern. When a person repeatedly and consistently refuses to leave the house and has little to no interactions with close friends and family, this is something to be worried about.

As humans, we are naturally social, so engaging with other people is good for our health. Healthy and loving relationships do wonders for your mental health. The feeling of closeness, acceptance, and support from people who matter to you can revoke feelings of despair and loneliness.

Maintaining loving relationships requires an effort from both parties. You can't expect someone to extend their friendship when you decline making plans with them. In the same way, you can't expect someone to fall in love with you when you show them no love in return. A difficult pill I had to swallow was the realization that I needed to make some real effort if I ever wanted my relationships to thrive.

I was single all throughout my twenties. I experienced love at only thirty years old, but it was worth the wait. But along the way, I had lost so much of my confidence and self-worth believing lies about myself. I somehow had made myself believe that the reason I was single was because I was unlovable.

Love isn't supposed to feel messy, but the idea of love contradicted my most inner feelings. It left me feeling devoid and undeserving. All the things love is and isn't only made me weary of receiving or returning love. The most difficult thing for me when writing this book was the biblical commandment of love. Depression once made me question the idea of experiencing love to its fullness.

The idea of love use to make my heart sink into despair and loneliness. The thought of love that wasn't real or lasting made me anxious and fearful. The idea of physical intimacy and sex made me resentful. Love felt lonely, and I turned away from experiencing it at every chance.

Whatever the meaning of love is, it's surely personal and I needed to understand it. Indeed, secular studies have contributed greatly to the knowledge of love and relationships, but I needed to first get rid of all my anxiety and the dysfunctional views about love I had in my mind. Regardless of my skewed knowledge of love, I rightfully longed for it, and I wanted to experience the kind that brings long-lasting happiness and joy. I opened the Bible and searched for love.

Love the Lord Your God

You shall love the Lord your God with all your heart
and with all your soul and with all your mind.

MATTHEW 22:37, NIV

IF LOVING GOD IS the greatest commandment of all, how do we mortal beings demonstrate our love to a divine being? Many religions have focused their practices and rituals on demonstrating their love to God, but what does the Bible say and how can it benefit us?

When Jesus was teaching the Pharisees, one of them asked, "'Which is the greatest commandment in the Law?' Jesus replied, 'You shall love the Lord your God with all your heart and with all your soul and with all your mind. This is the great and first commandment'" (Matt 22:36–37 NIV).

So what does it mean to love God with all our heart, soul, and mind, and why is it important?

Jesus made it clear and simple that the most important thing in our lives is to love God. He never said it will be simple or easy, but in all its clarity he means that love for God is essential to our living. There is no commandment more important than this. To love God with everything in us is the highest and greatest thing we can do in our lives. Jesus made a standard for this love. It isn't a kind of love that fades away in time or a kind of love that heightens during good times. It isn't a conditional love. It is a kind of love where we put our whole being into it. This isn't impractical or irrational, and God isn't asking too much. We are capable of loving God with our whole heart, soul, and mind if we choose to because God has created us to love the way he loves us. Our part in being created in the image of God is that we function in the likeness of him.

"We love because He first loved us" (1 John 4:19 NIV).

To love God with our heart, soul, and mind means to love God with all our innate emotions, desires, and thoughts. We need to dedicate and invest our being into the growth and development of that love. Without this love, life is meaningless. When we live for the pursuit of attaining this standard of love, this is where we find spiritual contentment. Our desire to grow in love and in relationship is fulfilled through our personal connection with God.

"May you experience the love of Christ, though it is too great to understand fully. Then you will be made complete with all the fullness of life and power that comes from God" (Eph 3:19 NLT).

God's love for us surpasses all understanding. It cannot be measured, nor can it be compared. We can never know what it amounts to. We can be confident in it—that though we were sinners, God sent his only Son for the atonement of our sins. This means that before we were even aware of our sinful nature, God granted us the gift of salvation. To love God doesn't begin with the knowledge of gaining salvation. To love God is to acknowledge our need for him. There comes a time in every believer's life where our worldly desires fade away and our primary need for God supersedes other needs.

When I was going through my longest stretch with my battle against depression, my need for connection and relationship far exceeded the emotional and mental turmoil in my heart and mind. Before anything, I longed for God. I needed his love, his care, and his promises. I needed God to come through for me in whichever way he deemed fit. I wanted him to part the sea, tear down walls for me, send fire raining from the heavens—whatever it was, I wanted him to show me that he was present and able in my life. My desperation for God to pull me out of my drowning state became obvious to people. A short while later, people started commenting on my physical appearance.

"What happened to you? You need to get some help. Like real medical help!"

There's nothing wrong with getting help; in fact, I did get help and it was what I needed. But medicine could not and cannot fill the void in my heart.

My mid- and late twenties were my most difficult years. I was single, struggling with my career, and unaware of my symptoms of depression and anxiety, and most days I felt lost and insecure. Rejection only made things worse. I felt unloved and unwanted. There has even been a time when I thought and felt that if people had rejected me, then maybe God had rejected me as well. I'd attend church and hear sermons about God's great love, and my heart would sink. I would think, "Does God really love me?"

I started saving Bible verses that reminded me of God's love and would read them every time I felt a sting of insecurity.

Bible verses kept reminding me that I was his child, loved and adored regardless of how I felt or how people treated me. I believe in who God says he is. He is love and he is enough. To know God loved me gave me a sense of security and belonging. This love gave me the will to live with hope, faith, and confidence. I believe I am never alone in Christ. He is with me and his love abides inside of me, and I love him back.

A passage that affirms the love of God is Rom 8:35–37: "Can anything ever separate us from Christ's love? Does it mean he no longer loves us if we have trouble or calamity, or if we are persecuted, or hungry, or destitute, or in danger, or threatened with death? . . . No, despite all these things, overwhelming victory is ours through Christ, who loved us" (NLT).

Regardless of my circumstances, this verse assures me that Jesus loves and accepts me just the way I am. *My* feelings, on the other hand, may keep changing according to my circumstances. At times I feel emotionally stable and become rational, and at other times, heartache and problems make me emotionally numb. It affects the confidence I have in God. Doubt settles in and blurs the faith and belief I have in him, but despite my feelings, Jesus loves me.

The word *love* appears in the Bible hundreds of times. It is the foundation for Christian belief. Jesus taught it, lived it, and died for it. He is the embodiment of what true love is. It isn't just in his character to love—the Bible says he *is* love. God cannot *not* love someone, simply because he is love.

Has there ever been a time where you doubted God's love for you? Like Gideon, have you questioned, "but if the Lord is with us, why has all this happened to us? (Judg 6:13 NIV). When pain and suffering sets us on a difficult path, we often wonder if God really loves us. If so, why is all this happening to me? Have circumstances around you made you doubt if God is really on your side?

These thoughts—like the ones Gideon and I had—are only human, but our pain and difficult circumstances are not an indicator of God's love for us. Jesus said, "In this world you will have trouble. But take heart! I have overcome the world" (John 16:33 NIV).

Jesus acknowledged that we will go through times of trouble in this world, but with him in our lives, he has promised we can overcome it because he has overcome the world (problems/sin in this world). Jesus teaches us that regardless of what we go through, we ought to love God. This is his commandment to all who believe in him, and it is a commandment I intend to keep close to my heart.

In times of praise and happiness, we need to love God. In hardship and troubling times, we need to love him the very same way. Chronic mental illness can cause us to harbor a lot of resentment from the frustration of having little to no control over our thoughts and emotions. On days we feel down and sad, and when worry and fear has us questioning our purpose and our mental-health state, we can resort to developing a close relation with God instead of getting frustrated and confused. God can be a father, a friend, and a confidant to you. It's easy to be grateful to God in the good times. It's the difficult times where our faith is tested. When God seems quiet and when he says no, love and trust him as if he had said yes! At all times and in all situations, our commitment to love God intensely, sincerely, lovingly, and passionately is the greatest commandment.

Bible Verses to Remember

*For God so loved the world that he gave his
one and only Son, that whoever believes in
him shall not perish but have eternal life.*
John 3:16, NIV

*And we know that in all things God works
for the good of those who love him, who have
been called according to his purpose.*
Rom 8:28, NIV

I have loved you with an everlasting love.
Jer 31:3, NIV

I trust in God's unfailing love forever and ever.
Ps 52:8, NIV

*And so we know and rely on the love God
has for us. God is love. Whoever lives in
love lives in God, and God in them.*
1 John 4:16, NIV

*Love the Lord your God with all your heart
and with all your soul and with all your
strength and with all your mind.*
Luke 10:27, NIV

*And I am convinced that nothing can ever separate us
from God's love. Neither death nor life, neither angels nor
demons, neither our fears for today nor our worries about
tomorrow—not even the powers of hell can separate us
from God's love. No power in the sky above or in the
earth below . . . will ever be able to separate us from the
love of God that is revealed in Christ Jesus our Lord.*
Rom 8:38–39, NIV

Love Others

Love one another. As I have loved you, so you must love one another.

JOHN 13:34, NIV

BEING SINGLE ALL THROUGHOUT my twenties had really took a toll on my confidence and self-worth. Like I mentioned, facing rejection even made me think that God had rejected me as well, and when I was feeling down and blue because of depression, this feeling only made me think the worst.

"It's because of me. I am the reason why I'm so single and alone."

"All those things that people say of me must be true."

"Will I ever be happy?"

I hate being insecure, and for so long, insecurity was like a shadow following me around, especially on the brightest of days. When the sun shone, it became even more difficult to ignore it.

Insecurity is a disease, but for those living with a chronic mental illness, it can brutally beat you down. I had all these misconceptions of mental health in my mind I couldn't shake off. I thought that if only things went the way they should or someone reacted to me the way they should, then I wouldn't feel that way!

After I was medicated, I realized that my mind was oddly calm, a little more than usual. Unwanted thoughts, especially those of a negative and sexual nature, would never even cross my mind. My emotions were stable. My random emotional shifts and mood swings from happiness to sadness or contentment to feeling troubled were a thing of the past. Today when I look back and think of those moments when I felt so worthless and dejected—when I barely could look forward to anything—I realize it was never because of me, my singleness, other people, or even God. It was just depression.

Depression, not God or other people, made me feel worthless. Anxiety robbed me of my sleep and peace—it wasn't because God had left me to suffer. My mental state was a result of the Fall and not because God had intended for mankind to live with pain and suffering. Rejection is only something we go through—it isn't personal, and it was definitely not because of me. (If people tell you it's because of you, they say it from a place of personal pain and shortcomings.) Depression made me lose interest in socializing, and it made me wonder if they even cared for me or if I should care for them in return. These were the lies depression made me believe!

All of these lies were not close to reality. I love the people in my life and I'm grateful for each one of them. They each played a big or small role in adding happiness and joy to my life, and I thank God for all of them. I pray to God all the time to give me the wisdom and the knowledge to love them in the way he would want me to.

A Bible verse that kept me searching for meaning and understanding is Mark 12:31: "Love your neighbor as yourself" (NIV).

"Neighbor" doesn't literally mean people who live close to you. Here, Jesus meant all of mankind—your enemies and allies, your friends and foes.

As I examined myself on whether or not I weigh high on the scale of showing and giving love, it felt weightless.

I don't think I've ever verbally and emotionally allowed myself to wholly receive love, let alone extend love to each and every person I meet. I even decided in a few instances to forgo writing about love, since I felt like I had none to express.

When asked about love, people can have contradicting associations drawn from personal experiences. Someone who is hurt and betrayed in love can have a more broken-down definition of love as compared to someone who has healed from hurt. So what is love from a universal standpoint?

Love is the only form of feeling that is supposedly universally agreed upon. Love is good. Love brings out the best in people. Love can melt a heart of stone. Love gives life purpose. But if love feels messy and awkward, like it did for me and a lot of other people, how can you live to experience the joys of love?

"Love is patient and kind. Love is not jealous or boastful or proud or rude. It does not demand its own way. It is not irritable, and it keeps no record of being wronged. It does not rejoice about injustice but rejoices whenever the truth wins out. Love never gives up, never loses faith, is always hopeful, and endures through every circumstance" (1 Cor 13:4–7 NLT).

This eye-opening verse was my point of reference. It teaches what love is and what it's not supposed to be. When having an indecisive feeling about extending love toward someone, remember that love can be platonic and friendly. The verse above is a reminder that we can all show love and care toward someone.

Love is having patience with someone who has exasperated you. Love is showing kindness to someone in need. Love is not getting jealous of your loved ones or keeping scores of your spouse. Love is not giving up on someone—instead, it demonstrates faith, hope, and endurance through every circumstance.

This kind of love means having godly traits. This kind of love is true and genuine. This kind of love matures you. This kind of love is your compass for life. This kind of love is the base of all healthy relationships. This is feeling and knowing you have loved.

Love must not be conditional. If someone fails to show you patience and kindness and all the love in the Corinthians verse, it does not mean that you do the same. Love is not showing up only when the same is extended toward you. In fact, love is most felt in the direst of situations.

The Bible says that for those who love, this is where God is present.

"God is love. Whoever lives in love lives in God, and God in them" (1 John 4:16 NIV).

God is love, and he who loves has God in them. God dwells in those who love him and others. We receive love through our relationship with God, and we experience love through our relationships with people. Love is so important to God that he made it a commandment. To love God and other people is the principal commandment for all Christians. Without love, the Bible says we have gained nothing.

"If I could speak all the languages of earth and of angels, but didn't love others, I would only be a noisy gong or a clanging cymbal. If I had the gift of prophecy, and if I understood all of God's secret plans and possessed all knowledge, and if I had such faith that I could move mountains, but didn't love others, I would be nothing. If I gave everything I have to the poor and even sacrificed my body, I could boast about it; but if I didn't love others, I would have gained nothing" (1 Cor 13:1–3 NLT).

In other words, if I could speak in the most eloquent of ways—one that could sway a lover or move a nation, one that could have power over decisions or that would be music to your ears—but didn't love, I would only be like a gong that echoes nothing but noise.

A person could have gifts and talents bestowed on them and use them all for benefit, but if he didn't have love, he would be nothing. Even if one gave to charity but didn't love, he would still be nothing.

Love is the most precious commodity in the eyes of God. Before anything, God expects you to love.

Bible Verses to Remember

*And over all these virtues put on love, which
binds them all together in perfect unity.*
Col 3:14, NIV

*Above all, love each other deeply, because
love covers over a multitude of sins.*
1 Pet 4:8, NIV

Love Others

*Finally, all of you, be like-minded, be sympathetic,
love one another, be compassionate and humble.*
1 Pet 3:8, NIV

*Owe nothing to anyone—except for your obliga-
tion to love one another. If you love your neighbor,
you will fulfill the requirements of God's law.*
Rom 13:8, NLT

*No one has ever seen God; but if we love one another,
God lives in us and his love is made complete in us.*
1 John 4:12, NIV

*Dear friends, let us continue to love one an-
other, for love comes from God. Anyone who
loves is a child of God and knows God.*
1 John 4:7, NLT

Promises of God

For no matter how many promises God has
made, they are "Yes" in Christ.

2 CORINTHIANS 1:20, NIV

DESPITE LIVING WITH DEPRESSION, I never let it control my life. I was able to lead a very normal life. I went to college and got a master's degree, was able to secure jobs and have a good network of friends and colleagues, and led a normal social life, but mentally, none of this came easily.

Most days, I would drag myself out of bed. I would go for days and weeks without sleep, which in turn caused me to feel paranoid and dazed, but in every instance of anxiety or panic, no matter how severe, I clung to the promises of God.

"'For I know the plans I have for you,' declares the Lord, 'plans to prosper you and not to harm you, plans to give you hope and a future' (Jer 29:11 NIV).

This verse gave me hope when it didn't feel like there was any left. This verse turned me into a warrior of faith. Even if it didn't feel like God was there for me, I chose to believe he was. Even if it didn't feel like I was living an abundant life, I chose to believe God had plans for me. For every doubt I had, there was a biblical promise banishing it. For every fear and anxiety I went through, there was a biblical promise condemning it with truth and confirmation.

I had no reason to anticipate a bleak future. God's promises to his people stand over time. They don't change because he remains the same. The same God who liberated a nation, brought down walls, parted the sea, and humbled the proud is the same God I believe in. I simply ran out of reasons to not trust God.

I cannot emphasis the need I had for God to come through for me. Of course, now I understand that this need was adulterated by my depression. My need turned into desperation. If there's anyone out there reading this right now who feels or has felt the same way, I encourage you to get help. Sometimes, the right medication is just what you need to feel normal again.

A lot of people may think this is normal. The need for God is normal. I can assure you that I still need God, with medications or without. I'll always need God. There's nothing the world can offer that will replace my longing for God. The only difference is that my longing and need for God doesn't make me feel empty and alone anymore. It makes me feel safe and assured.

There are countless promises of God to his people written in the Bible—promises of love, hope, guidance, freedom, provision, forgiveness, redemption, and eternal life. We are not talking about the promises in the old or new covenant or about the Old and New Testament; we are talking about the promises of God to his people found throughout the Scriptures. These promises help us in both the smallest and the most significant moments of our lives. These are promises that guide us through uncertainty, doubt, fear, loss, and heartache, and in turn instill confidence, assurance, trust, renewal, and fulfillment. These are promises that reveal to us the character, sovereignty, and greatness of God, and at the same time remind us of his love, grace, and presence. Some people may think God fulfills his promises based on people's faith, but this isn't biblical. It is God's will that all be saved, and it is according to his will how his blessings are bestowed upon people's lives and to whom.

"The Lord is not slow in keeping his promise, as some understand slowness. Instead he is patient with you, not wanting anyone to perish, but everyone to come to repentance" (2 Pet 3:9 NIV).

Whether we deny God and all that he is, say we don't believe in the existence of God, or doubt his presence with us, God has already established a covenant relationship with us. Before creation and before the Fall, God had an eternal plan of redemption for us and with it, promises that exceed more than sustenance and survival for human beings. He lovingly calls us, his children and mortal creations, and we are granted admission to a personal relationship with him, one where we are not entitled to rewards but where we can inherit blessings, salvation, healing, growth, and prosperity.

"From one man He made every nation of men, that they should inhabit the whole earth; and He determined their appointed times and the boundaries of their lands. God intended that they would seek Him and perhaps reach out for Him and find Him, though He is not far from each one of us. For in Him we live and move and have our being" (Acts 17: 26–28 BSB).

Bible Verses to Remember

So do not fear, for I am with you; do not be dismayed,
for I am your God. I will strengthen you and help you;
I will uphold you with my righteous right hand.
Isa 41:10, NIV

Do not be anxious about anything, but in every situation, by prayer and petition, with
thanksgiving, present your requests to God.
Phil 4:6, NIV

As far as the east is from the west, so far has
he removed our transgressions from us.
Ps 103:12, NIV

As Scripture says, "Anyone who believes
in him will never be put to shame."
Rom 10:11, NIV

He heals the brokenhearted and binds up their wounds.
Ps 147:3, TPT

Promises of God

*I instruct you in the way of wisdom and
lead you along straight paths.*
Prov 4:11, NIV

*"I will not cause pain without allowing some-
thing new to be born," says the Lord.*
Isa 66:9, NCV

*You will seek me and find me when
you seek me with all your heart*
Jer 29:13, NIV

Purpose

*"For I know the plans I have for you," declares the Lord, "plans to
prosper you and not to harm you, plans to give you hope and a future."*

JEREMIAH 29:11, NIV

WHEN YOU ASK PEOPLE what they think of God's purpose for
their lives, you'll come across many opinions. Most Christians
acknowledge that God has a plan for their lives, but how this plan
plays out in their lives and who has control or say in it depends
on several factors aside from God. Some may even say that living
a life according to God's plan is a killjoy, as if God has restricted
them from enjoying life or living life to their greatest potential.
Others may argue that God's purpose doesn't fall into their hands
overnight. No one can rightly know what's God's purpose is for
them, and we should just wing it. Some may say God's purpose is
found through some dramatic or spiritual experience that can only
happen in a person's life once in a lifetime.

There is no definitive guideline for God's intended purpose in
every person's life. One way we can know about our life's purpose
is knowing what God has created us to be. When we think of a
purpose, we think of something significant, one that gives meaning to our lives.

A lot of people feel down and depressed or ruminate on anxious and negative thoughts when they feel they lack purpose and

direction in life. Many say they feel unworthy or they don't have much to live for. For a brief period of time, I was fearful of my future. Depression made it look gloomy, dark, and hopeless. There wasn't much to look forward to. My days were just passing by with little to no hope or joy. My mind hovered over the thought that I wasn't enough. This specific period of my life is something I never wish to revisit—and sadly, a lot of people have had days like mine.

People with a sense of purpose and meaning in their lives tend to cope better on a number of measures of mental health and mental well-being. Finding what you think gives purpose does not mean all your mental-health problems will disappear. Finding something you like or even love will add to your sense of meaning and value in life. A misconception believed by many is that life will feel fulfilled once you achieve your intended purpose or worse, that your depression will instantly disappear once you realize your greatest purpose in life. The truth is that depression, anxiety, and any chronic illness can be managed better when you successfully shift your attention to things that add value to your life, rather than ruminating on feelings and thoughts caused by depression and anxiety. Depression isn't going to fade away once you hit a milestone in life. Things are not going to get better once you get married or once you finally get the promotion you deserve. Things will only get better when you decide to make them better.

For many people, a purpose can be a lot of things. You can be at the beginning of a successful career or in the midst of a midlife crisis, but our search for meaning and purpose in life is endless.

Some say the purpose in life is love—that to love and be loved is the highest reward in life. Some say it is happiness—that to achieve personal happiness and be able to make others happy gives a great sense of well-being. To some it is more tangible: Purpose is connected to vocation—a meaningful and satisfying job or getting married and starting a family of one's own is what gives life meaning. Some may spend most of their days trying to achieve something they think is their purpose in life.

How do you find purpose in life? What does the Bible say about life's purpose? Let's go back to where it all started.

"Then God said, 'Let us make mankind in our image, in our likeness'" (Gen 1:26 NIV).

This passage does not mean that God is in human form, but rather that humans are created in the image of God in their moral, spiritual, and intellectual nature. Just as children bear the image and likeness of their parents, God created male and female to bear his likeness. All humans are therefore created in the image of God for a purpose. The image of God underlines the dignity, value, and worth of human beings. We are creations who reflect our Creator.

People with mental illness are no less valuable before God. The Bible says God is close to those who are brokenhearted. It does not discriminate against people. You are not inferior or an outcast for suffering from an illness that has little to no physical symptoms. People may be unable to predict your situation, but God can. He knows the outcome and the path you're on, and he cares for you nonetheless. Though tainted by sin, we are still prized in his eyes. We are considered worthy of salvation and are given the promise of a life that can be measured as fullness. God sent his son Jesus Christ for that very purpose.

"Be imitators of God, therefore, as beloved children, and walk in love, just as Christ loved us and gave Himself up for us as a fragrant sacrificial offering to God" (Eph 5:1–2 BSB).

The Bible clearly instructs us to be people who copy the behavior and character of God. If anyone says we can never be godly or aspire to have godly characteristics in our lives, they are going against Scripture. Men and women were created in the image of God to reflect who God is and what he's like.

The image of God in humans was disfigured in the Fall. When Adam and Eve sinned, the moral purity of God in us was lost, and our sinful character did not reflect God's holiness. When sin crept into our lives, we lost the whole likeness of God in us, but through Jesus we can restore our sinful nature through communion with God. Although we are never whole in nature, like God is—and some aspects of that image is lost or distorted—yet people, Christians or not, still bear the image of God.

Purpose

We were created to love like God loves us. We were created to have fellowship and relationship with God and one another, just like God with us, the Father with Jesus, and the Father and Jesus with the Holy Spirit. We were created on purpose and for a purpose. Our longing for significance and desire for meaning are part of being created in the image of God.

Our individual purpose can be anything to different people. We can find purpose in our gifts and talents. God created us with unique qualifications where we can contribute to help or be of service to others, thereby fulfilling our sense of meaning in life. We can use our God-given passions to add meaning to our personal lives. Since we are created for a purpose, living a purposeless life only defeats our most primitive longing. It's the knowledge that we are not living to our greatest potential that weighs us down. This can affect us mentally and spiritually. A loss of meaning and purpose can remove from a person the power to cope with life's difficulties. Depression can cause a person to lose the sense of importance and significance before given to things once held valuable. Depression can affect not only a person's mental state but also relationships with people close to them.

Finding what can add meaning and purpose to your life in the midst of a mental illness can help you cope and manage it far better. Attending church services has helped reduce my level of anxiety and depression. I love going to church. It is my spiritual getaway. During my most difficult struggle with depression, church was the one thing I would always look forward to. Praying and worship helped alleviate emotional distress. Of course, there were times when all I wanted was to stay home tucked in bed. Depression is a roller coaster!

The best and most biblical way of living a more meaningful life is to find joy in our God-given gifts and use them to do good.

"In his grace, God has given us different gifts for doing certain things well. So if God has given you the ability to prophesy, speak out with as much faith as God has given you. If your gift is serving others, serve them well. If you are a teacher, teach well. If your gift is to encourage others, be encouraging. If it is giving, give generously. If God has given you leadership ability, take the responsibility seriously. And if you have a gift for showing kindness to others, do it gladly" (Rom 12:6–8 NLT).

I started writing while I was working at a digital agency in Mumbai. They encouraged me to write and I started loving every second of it. My writing started spilling into my personal life. At first, I wasn't sure what I was writing. It sounded amateurish, but some had a poetic rhyme. I love music, particularly worship songs. I would watch lyric videos on YouTube because I loved listening and reading the words to a song. For me, worship songs are meant for healing, rest, and connection. Soon, this became something that interested me. I started composing lyrical poems and essays, and what I thought was originally going to be for blogs started forming into a book. Words kept bleeding onto pages.

Writing became my escape. I quickly found peace in my writing. Psychiatrists and counselors do advise their patients to write or journal their thoughts as a means of coping with depression and anxiety. You can do the same if it helps. Find something you love or something that ignites your passion and use it to add to your purpose and sense of meaning in your life. I don't consider myself to be an author. I never grew up thinking, "One day I'm gonna write a book!"—but here I am, sharing the highs and lows of my life, hoping it can inspire someone out there to live beyond the hurt, pain, and loneliness of depression.

Bible Verses to Remember

Delight yourself in the Lord, and he will
give you the desires of your heart.
Ps 37:4, ESV

And we know that in all things God works
for the good of those who love him, who have
been called according to his purpose.
Rom 8:28, NIV

Purpose

*If you abide in me, and my words abide in you, ask
whatever you wish, and it will be done for you.*
John 15:7, ESV

Faith

Faith is confidence in what we hope for and assurance about what we do not see.

HEBREWS 11:1, NIV

MY FAITH IN GOD has gotten me through some of the scariest moments of my life. Every time I felt overwhelmed by negativity and circumstances outside my control, my faith in God would comfort me. It took a while for me to accept the fact that I had a mental problem to deal with. Prior to my realization and acceptance, I was confused and disturbed with my own thoughts, and on most days, I was unaware of my random shifts in mood and energy. Some days, my mind would just drift aimlessly to past events and scenarios I wouldn't recall on my normal days. I'd fixate on such scenarios for days to exhaustion. Replaying conversations in my head was my most destructive habit. A few times, my mother caught me smiling or frowning at myself. I failed miserably to break this habit on my own. Later on, I was put on medication and for the first time in a very long time, I experienced quietness.

There have been too many instances where I questioned God. When overwhelmed with hopelessness, one is made to question one's own worth and value as a human being. A lot of these questions were directed at God.

"Do you care for my health and happiness?"

"When are you going to come through for me?"

"Am I unworthy of love?"

These were just a few of my frequently asked questions. As I grew older and more exposed to life's experiences, and my thoughts were shaped by circumstances, my questions about life and faith change. I wanted to hold on to that childlike faith that didn't hesitate a moment to believe. At moments when I felt overwhelmed with emotions and terrorized from my restless mind, I sought refuge in the Bible. God's promises to Jacob became my source of renewed faith.

"Do not be afraid, for I have ransomed you. I have called you by name; you are mine. When you go through deep waters, I will be with you. When you go through rivers of difficulty, you will not drown. When you walk through the fire of oppression, you will not be burned up; the flames will not consume you. For I am the LORD, your God, the Holy One of Israel, your Savior" (Isa 43:1–3 NLT).

God is so many things to me and I didn't want to live without him. I wanted to trust him wholeheartedly. I wanted to believe that his promises would see me through my days. I wanted to experience them in every way. What I needed more was spiritual fulfillment. I knew depression and anxiety were affecting my life and I needed to make better choices for my mental well-being, but first, I needed God. I decided to make God my first priority.

Sadly, I've come across many people who talk down someone else's faith and belief. The fact that some people show so much hatred toward someone's faith astounds me. I have been on the receiving end of hate many times. Often it was by people I considered close. This is something common and most Christians can testify to it, but Jesus teaches us that we only gain from insults and mockery.

"God blesses you when people mock you and persecute you and lie about you and say all sorts of evil things against you because you are my followers" (Matt 5:11 NLT).

You have nothing to be ashamed of. If you believe in God and Jesus Christ as your Savior, live like it. Jesus was mocked when He was crucified, but he loved and accepted the very people who nailed him to the cross, so how important it is for us to demonstrate the very same love and acceptance to others. I am not ashamed of what Christ did for me. The very same faith saw me through the darkest moments in my life. I wouldn't be living carefree and content if it wasn't for the goodness of God. The promises he made to me held me together, and the very same promises prompted me to write this book. My hope is that this book can help others like me who are searching for healing during a trying time. I pray they find comfort and renewal in these biblical promises.

"Jesus replied, 'Anyone who loves me will obey my teaching. My Father will love them, and we will come to them and make our home with them'" (John 14:23 NIV).

Bible Verses to Remember

And without faith it is impossible to please God, because anyone who comes to him must believe that he exists and that he rewards those who earnestly seek him.
Heb 11:6, NIV

Be on guard. Stand firm in the faith.
Be courageous. Be strong.
1 Cor 16:13, NLT

And Jesus answered them, "Have faith in God. Truly, I say to you, whoever says to this mountain, 'Be taken up and thrown into the sea,' and does not doubt in his heart, but believes that what he says will come to pass, it will be done for him. Therefore I tell you, whatever you ask in prayer, believe that you have received it, and it will be yours."
Mark 11:22–24, ESV

That your faith might not rest in the wisdom of men but in the power of God.
1 Cor 2:5, ESV

Prayers

This is the confidence we have in approaching God: that
if we ask anything according to his will, he hears us.

1 JOHN 5:14, NIV

PRAYER IS A CONVERSATION, not mere communication. Prayer is receiving more than asking. Prayer is personal and spontaneous, not tactful and scheduled. Prayer is showing up with all your insecurities and imperfections to an all-perfect God.

Prayer has been so many things to me—it makes me feel connected to God in a raw, painful, and honest way that always feels freeing. Sometimes prayer has been rather therapeutic, but this is not to say that prayer is simply for therapeutic self-analysis. Of course, these are prayers said within the safety of my bedroom walls. Prayer can be messy at a whole other level. When anxiety strikes, I wonder about God's reaction to my gloomy and sullen words. Would he sigh at me? I would. I—a creation of God, loved and adored—thought I had the luxury to pour out my temperamental emotions into words, and I expected him to deal with it.

God is my spiritual Father. When I couldn't go to anyone, I turned to God. My prayers were never poised, eloquent, or well articulated. They were complaints, apologies, and a lot of questions. I would list some examples, but I'm too embarrassed. I have sometimes turned into a little girl throwing random tantrums because I thought God wasn't paying attention to me. Looking back, my expectations from God were close to those of a child expecting candy from a parent after a long absence. I never received any candy. I received something more valuable—I received healing.

If you grew up in a Christian home, you might have been taught the importance of prayer. I was taught to pray every morning before getting out of bed and every night before going to bed. I followed this and was able to stick with it for a while. But I soon found myself saying the same old prayer and never felt closer to God. Prayer became a habit, just words uttered by a little girl to a God who is bigger than anything.

If God would move mountains for me, I couldn't dare to believe what my future would hold when my prayers were fulfilled. My heart sank when reality hit. Prayers don't work that way. You might say a thousand words, throw in the fanciest vocabulary, and never miss a day, but if your prayers don't align with God and his will for you, prayers remain just words.

I decided to quit supplication and start intercession. Little did I know that God is one for intercession. I stood bravely in the face of adversity and interceded for my well-being. I wasn't going to let depression and anxiety win this one.

One thing people ask is why pray in the first place if God already knows what you're going to say. Prayer is commanded by God. It is for his glory and for our own benefit. First, prayer creates a burning desire to seek, love, and serve God as we become accustomed to go to him first and foremost for every need and situation we go through. Secondly, prayer protects our hearts from temptation and fleshly desires. Lastly, prayer prepares us for receiving the benefits God will bless us with in his timing with gratitude, obedience, and wisdom.

You may find yourself in a place where you're not quite sure where to begin in prayer, but take comfort in the fact that God already know our hearts and our unspoken petitions. When we find ourselves in this too-familiar place and we are unable to express our thoughts, emotions, and feelings, don't be discouraged, for the Spirit of God will intercede for us. When we don't know how to pray or what to pray, the Bible says the Spirit will intervene on our behalf in accordance with God's will.

"In the same way, the Spirit helps us in our weakness. We do not know what we ought to pray for, but the Spirit himself intercedes for us through wordless groans. And he who searches our hearts knows the mind of the Spirit, because the Spirit intercedes for God's people in accordance with the will of God" (Rom 8:26–27 NIV).

One of the most common things that can happen to anyone—and something that has happened to me—are unwanted, intrusive thoughts that cause distress, anxiety, and depression. Something you need to keep in mind is to not let intrusive thoughts be the focus of your prayers and meditations. Let your prayers and meditation be a source of healing rather than venting. God already knows what you're dealing with. He knows the fear and anxiety it has caused you. He hears your desperate cry for help. Prayers don't have to be constant supplication for healings, solutions, remedies and provisions. Instead, they can be prayers of thanksgiving with humility for the healings, solutions, remedies, and provisions that are yet to be received.

"Do not be anxious about anything, but in every situation, by prayer and petition, with thanksgiving, present your requests to God" (Phil 4:6 NIV).

Meditating does not mean you sit with the Bible day and night; rather, you apply God's word in your life 24/7. Think about it—if someone religiously prays day and night but does not live by God's word, what is the purpose of their prayer? Likewise, you may read the Bible daily, but if you don't live by it, it serves no purpose in your life. You read and apply God's word and commandments to your life, mind, and heart.

Prayers can be a conversation between you and God where you tell God about your feelings and your problems, your praise and adoration, your confession and repentance, your thanksgiving and gratitude, and your worship and devotion. You hear God tell you he's taken the problem off your hands when Christ died for us, and he's given you all you need simply because you have glorified him in your most private life.

Negative thoughts, anxieties, insecurities, loss, grief, sickness, financial problems, broken families, and poverty are just obstacles on the way. You cannot get rid of them—you will have to go through all of them, but the prize beyond the finished line is already yours.

"Therefore I tell you, whatever you ask for in prayer, believe that you have received it, and it will be yours" (Mark 11:24 NIV).

The Bible teaches us how to pray. The disciples asked Jesus to teach them about prayer. Jesus then instructs them about how to pray, as is written in Matt 6:5–8:

> When you pray, don't be like the hypocrites who love to pray publicly on street corners and in the synagogues where everyone can see them. I tell you the truth, that is all the reward they will ever get. But when you pray, go away by yourself, shut the door behind you, and pray to your Father in private. Then your Father, who sees everything, will reward you. When you pray, don't babble on and on as the Gentiles do. They think their prayers are answered merely by repeating their words again and again. Don't be like them, for your Father knows exactly what you need even before you ask him! (NLT)

Notice that in this passage, Jesus does not give instructions on which words you should choose when praying but simply points out the hypocrisy of people when praying in public. Jesus wants us to have an intimacy and closeness with God when conversing with him. He wants personal, genuine petitions to be presented to God—petitions that are according to his will, petitions for daily provision, forgiveness for those who do us wrong, and petitions to deliver us from evil.

Bible Verses to Remember

Ask and it will be given to you; seek and you will find; knock and the door will be opened to you.
Matt 7:7, NIV

If you abide in me, and my words abide in you, ask whatever you wish, and it will be done for you.
John 15:7, ESV

But when you pray, go into your room, close the door and pray to your Father, who is unseen. Then your Father, who sees what is done in secret, will reward you.
Matt 6:6, NIV

Do not be anxious about anything, but in every situation, by prayer and petition, with thanksgiving, present your requests to God. And the peace of God, which transcends all understanding, will guard your hearts and your minds in Christ Jesus.
Phil 4:6–7, NIV

Now faith is confidence in what we hope for and assurance about what we do not see.
Heb 11:1, NIV

I prayed to the LORD, and he answered me.
Ps 34:4, NLT

Trust

*Trust in the Lord with all your heart and lean not on
your own understanding; in all your ways submit to
him, and he will make your paths straight.*

PROVERBS 3:5-6, NIV

FOR THE LONGEST TIME, I was afraid to confront my feelings. I've
always been aware that anxiety and depression are fairly common,
especially in adolescents. I waited for years, thinking it was just
a phase I was going through, that soon it would all be over, and
that all I needed was the will to power through what seemed to
be the most difficult years of adulthood. I waited and hoped for
better days, but then I hit rock bottom. When I was going through
my toughest time in my battle with depression, I felt like I was
slowly losing my sanity. On the most distressing of days, my mind
was no longer mine. I went on for days without sleep, and most
nights I would lay awake in bed replaying conversations, possible
scenarios, and unwanted thoughts of an immoral nature. I would
lose my appetite and interest in daily activities. These strenuous
days that turned into months made me have delusional and paranoid thoughts.

I hated going to bed and I dreaded facing each new day, and it
became lonelier and more exhausting by the minute. I started losing interest in activities and relationships. I'd have unpredictable

emotional reactions, and often I'd feel a mixture of two or more emotions at the same time. One moment I'd feel happy and content, and in a second I'd sink into feelings of sadness and depression. One moment I'd feel ashamed and defeated for having depression, and in a blink I'd feel hopeful and driven to overcome it.

At times when I was out with a friend or companion, I'd find myself having conflicting feelings about our conversations and relationship, and often I would wrongly translate this as actual feelings I had toward the particular person. I tried to *control* or hold in my feelings. I thought that if I had better control of my emotions, I would be able to manage stress more efficiently and in turn reduce my level of anxiety. I tried to confide in people close to me, but each time I'd panic and fail to express the severity or authenticity of what I was experiencing. Every time I confided in people close to me about my struggle with anxiety, my attacks of sleep paralysis, or my paranoia, I could never find the right words. I'd stumble through it with depictions of personal struggles that were either too insignificant or too consequential.

Anxiety and accumulated stress can cause someone to distrust their own feelings. Overwhelming emotions can lead someone to suppress their true feelings. When you lack the confidence to express your feelings, just the thought of expressing them can feel terrifying. Some may fear being misjudged or being frowned upon. In my case, I was too afraid to come to terms with my feelings. Suppressing my feelings did not help me cope with what I was going through. In fact, this worsened it. I was continuously thinking of ways I could express them. I played scenarios in my head of conversations I would have with parents and family members about my endless battle with depression and anxiety.

Confiding in people you trust about your mental state does help. It's important to not have high hopes and expectations from your conversations. You may not get the reactions or assurances you expect, simply because they may lack the know-how or the ability to give you plausible explanations and solutions. However, in most cases, people confide in others about their deepest and darkest feelings not because they seek explanations or solutions but rather because they are simply looking for support.

Looking back to when I was much younger, I empathize with the girl who tried to rally against her demons on her own. At that time, I was unaware about depression and anxiety and didn't know how to manage it, and I certainly didn't know how to talk about it. I simply accepted that I wasn't okay.

I made a habit of compartmentalizing my emotions so I wouldn't feel overwhelmed by them. The emotions that I thought were on top of my emotional pyramid had priority, and the rest followed. In theory, learning to have control over our feelings by separating them in order to avoid internal conflict feels good. Most of us would like to master the art of separating our emotional issues into "compartments," leaving them there for the time being, and *dealing* with them when the need arises. I was confident my emotions were managed and delegated into the right categories, but then the pyramid would all come down, and the emotions would pile up on each other and create a mixture of chaos.

The harm of leaving behind emotional issues is that they can build up and accumulate over time. Feelings are often withheld or suppressed over time due to the fear of losing control over them, the need to control your emotions, or, in a few cases, the reality that it is too daunting to fully recognize your own conflicting emotions. This can build up and cause stress, anxiety, and depression, and even have physical effects on your body.

Exhausted, I surrendered my control. As Ps 37:7 says, "Be still in the presence of the LORD, and wait patiently for him to act" (NLT).

I surrendered the need to have control over my emotions. Whenever I feel angry or frustrated, I acknowledge my anger or frustration and let it calm down naturally. If it becomes unsettling to hold on to my emotions, I take the initiative to talk to someone about my angry and frustrating feelings without justifying them or trying to reason through them. I tell them, "I'm been feeling angry and frustrated lately and I don't quite know why, but this is how I feel." Then I leave it there with willingness and acceptance.

Learning to let go of control over how I feel has reduced my stress considerably. I still feel conflicting emotions and thoughts. Sometime they spill into my conversations and reactions and even into my faith and belief, but I've learned to be still and not let emotions rule my life. Trusting God with my emotions has been the most rewarding lesson. It didn't happen overnight, and it sure wasn't easy. There were too many times when I felt hopeless, but surrendering to God seemed to be my only option, so I did it.

Over the course of time, my emotions have stabilized naturally, and I no longer feel the need to compartmentalize or manage them. Whenever my emotions "act up," I calm down and remind myself who is in control.

"Let go of your concerns! Then you will know that I am God" (Ps 46:10 GW).

Trust God when you don't understand, when things don't make sense or go your way. Trust is easier when you are confident about the outcome of a situation. The difficult times are when God wants you seek his ways rather than your own. They are the times when you fear the unknown or the past. It's when you cannot navigate emotional turbulence. It's during times of surrender. That's the time to trust a God who's bigger than any problem.

As humans, we question many things when it comes to our faith. The one question that keeps popping in my head is "What if I'm wrong about my belief?" God is not only faithful and kind. He is also a just and all-knowing God. When he created humans, he surely must have thought about me and all my conflicting feelings. The answers to any question you and I may have are all written in the Bible. Open it and read, or subscribe to a daily devotional or anything that can feed your spiritual knowledge.

Trust is a choice—a decision and an action. Choose to trust his words and not our own understanding.

Bible Verses to Remember

*The LORD is my strength and shield. I trust him with
all my heart. He helps me, and my heart is filled
with joy. I burst out in songs of thanksgiving.*
Ps 28:7, NLT

*Commit everything you do to the LORD.
Trust him, and he will help you.*
Ps 37:5, NLT

When I am afraid, I put my trust in you.
Ps 56:3, NIV

*But blessed is the one who trusts in the
Lord, whose confidence is in Him.*
Jer 17:7, NIV

Those who trust in the Lord will prosper.
Prov 28:25, NIV

*Those who trust in themselves are fools, but
those who walk in wisdom are kept safe.*
Prov 28:26, NIV

But now, Lord, what do I look for? My hope is in you.
Ps 39:7, NIV

*Be on your guard; stand firm in the
faith; be courageous; be strong.*
1 Cor 16:13, NIV

*I keep my eyes always on the Lord. With him
at my right hand, I will not be shaken.*
Ps 16:8, NIV

Heart & Mind

For as he thinks in his heart, so is he.

PROVERBS 23:7, NKJV

THE ABOVE PROVERB IS biblically and rationally true. You are shaped by what your heart desires.

When you desire good things, you live for the achievement of these good things, and the opposite is also true. We all desire things that make us feel secure: an ideal partner, money, success, happiness, stability, and living out our passion. Most people go for the social norm to attain these desires. We form relationships, fall in love, work for money and success, and invest in things that make us happy, and if you're lucky, all of this can be your passion.

For some, the fulfillment of these desires is unreachable or unattainable. Love and happiness can become difficult to achieve and even difficult to maintain. The biggest challenge for people is not knowing what makes them happy. They look for happiness in their jobs, spouses, material possessions, and spontaneous adventures. There is nothing wrong with having any of these things as part of life, but measuring your happiness based on them only leads to temporary bliss. Money is something we can never have enough of. No matter how much we earn, we want more. We think success equates to increasing our bank account balance. For some, we have deceived ourselves by allowing our passions to be monetized. The more money we're banking, the more we're living life to its best.

The heart can contradict the mind. You may desire for things, people, relationships, and personal achievements, but when it's difficult to achieve our desires, we allow our minds to be prisoners of the ever-elusive.

Unrealistic goals can cause a lot of general anxiety and depression. Adapting to life by letting go of these goals and setting a more realistic framework can make life so much sweeter. This is not to say we should quit and give up on achieving. Rather, we change our mindset regarding what achievement means to us.

Set goals that are achievable and good for you. Your ambition should be a testament to your talents, skills, intelligence, and creativity. Your work should bring you pride, appreciation, and security.

We are not left to live on earth and figure it out on our own; we are here to experience a purpose. We shouldn't confuse this purpose and equate it to meaning a life that is successful on our terms. Most of us feel abandoned by God because we think our lives don't add up to the often materialist expectations of what life should be like.

Happiness should not equate to a big, fancy house or a paycheck. Happiness can be contentment, optimism, self-care, and gratitude. Love does not have to be dependent on your partner and other people. Love can be acceptance, appreciation, care, and forgiveness. Success does not mean big bucks. It can be comfort, motivation, willingness, and balance. Fulfilling your passions does not mean you need recognition. Passion can be personal, fulfilling, charitable, and therapeutic.

Reshaping your life may change the way you think. Any change that happens in our life starts by changing the way we think. Be positive and nurturing toward yourself. Avoid external factors that feed negative thinking. Choose to have stronger control over which thoughts can run your life.

In his letter to the church of Philippians, Paul writes, "Finally, whatever is true, whatever is honorable, whatever is just, whatever is pure, whatever is lovely, whatever is commendable, if there is any excellence, if there is anything worthy of praise, think about these things" (Phil 4:8 NIV).

Let your mind be filled with thoughts, ideas, and desires that are positive, realistic, justified, and holy. If your thoughts are filled with destructive thinking, it leaves very little space for you to think straight. Destructive or negative thoughts can cause a lot of stress. Stress triggers anxiety and depression that can make the very little daily things in life challenging.

Problems arise when we allow external factors to have control over the way we think. When we allow people, social media, television, and magazines have influence over what we think, the way we feel will always be an outcome of what others think and not what we truly want to feel. People wish they could only change their circumstances, but real change happens when we change the narrative of our thoughts.

What happens when we allow our minds to think of only good things, as Paul described? We gain the promises of God.

"And the peace of God, which transcends all understanding, will guard your hearts and your minds in Christ Jesus" (Phil 4:7 NIV).

Bible Verses to Remember

Do not be conformed to this world, but be transformed by the renewal of your mind.
Rom 12:2, ESV

Create in me a clean heart, O God, and renew a right spirit within me.
Ps 51:10, ESV

Set your minds on things that are above, not on things that are on earth.
Col 3:2, ESV

In the Midst of It All

*Delight yourself in the Lord, and he will
give you the desires of your heart.*
Ps 37:4, ESV

*Above all else, guard your heart, for ev-
erything you do flows from it.*
Prov 4:23, NIV

Fear

For God hath not given us the spirit of fear; but of
power, and of love, and of a sound mind.

2 TIMOTHY 1:7, KJV

THERE IS A CLEAR distinction between fear and anxiety. Anxiety
is a generalized response to an unknown threat or internal conflict, whereas fear is focused on known, external danger. Fear
can be associated with a sudden urge of adrenaline, thoughts of
immediate danger, and a need to escape. Anxiety, on the other
hand, is feeling uncertain about what is about to happen or what
may or may not happen.

Our insecurities are usually irrational fears that may or may
not be serious. An insecurity is something we are afraid of experiencing, gaining, or loosing. Some are just surface level, like the
fear of making decisions, being alone, making new friends, having
intimate relationships, public speaking, illness, and so on. Some
involve the ego: rejection, success, failure, disapproval, intimacy,
loss of identity, and so on.

When I was younger, I experienced many difficulties with
sleeping at night. First, there was parasomnia, which happened
more than usual. The nature and frequency of it got worse throughout the years. My experience with parasomnia started in my early
teenage years and lasted till my midtwenties. This unusual sleep

behavior would happen in the early mornings when I was in between sleep and wakefulness. Suddenly my mind would wake me up to "someone" (an inhuman object) groping and touching me and my body going paralysed from the inability to move or call for help. These hands would change to limbs made of roots. I'd fight to wake up from it, only for it to happen again and again. I felt molested in my unconscious state.

Secondly, I had night terrors. I'd sometimes wake up in the middle of the night with a terrified feeling and my heart racing. Some nights, I would wake up thinking there was someone or something lurking in my room. These abnormal sleep behaviors troubled me greatly. I'd wake up to a feeling of helplessness, left to rationalize my thoughts. I'd pray and go about my normal day, and the same thing would happen again only a few months later. This took a toll on my mental and physical health.

This went on for years—up until my late twenties, when it all stopped. My psychiatrist said it was because I wasn't afraid anymore, but it all came with a price. Before all of it stopped, before I was put on medications, I hit rock bottom. For months I went without sleep, which made me have delusional and obsessive thoughts. I had grandiose thoughts about my personality and life, and even had beliefs associated with God that were unbiblical. I felt like it was up to God if he wished to fix me and my situation.

I went through an emotional roller coaster that never felt justified or even reasonable. I had random emotional outbursts, I fought with my parents, I didn't want to leave the house, and I isolated myself from friends and family. I stopped doing the things I love, like reading, listening to music, and praying, and became lazy about attending church.

Chronic fear can cause a lot of confusion. I felt emotions and thoughts that were unjustified and made no absolute sense. I spent my twenties thinking I was betrayed. I was left to feel like my mind and body were two separate entities that didn't belong to me. This caused a lot of fear, resentment, and anger, and most of it was directed at God. He was the reason I had all these issues and problems. He had created me—and he had created a broken girl.

This is how I felt for a long time. Exhausted, I told the doctor, "I just want all this to end and to be healthy!" I was put on medication and it gave me relief. Though the medications helped me, my heart longed for God. There was nothing I wanted more than to feel emotionally and mentally secure.

God says in 1 John 4:18 that "there is no fear in love, but perfect love casts out fear" (ESV).

This verse troubled me. It made me ask a lot of questions. One of them was the question of where I could find this perfect love.

If perfect love could drive out fear, it was obvious it didn't exist within me.

If fear and anxiety ruled my thoughts, was there a place for love?

The Bible says perfect love is only found in God and not in human relations. The question now remained: If I have love for God, why do I have fear?

Sin can cause people to fear. Fear keeps people away from freedom. Most people are afraid of their own mistakes, which in turn leads them to have little faith in the future. Other people's sin can also instill a sense of fear in our lives. If you suffered abuse or trauma as a child or adult, fear can creep into your life.

Fear has many faces. You're scared of the future or everyday situations—that is anxiety. You're scared of the unknown—that's worry. You're scared of feeling joy—that's depression. Negative feelings and habits start somewhere, and that place is fueled by fear.

Fear keeps people in bondage. Fear keeps people from living hopefully and joyfully. When God intends to give you a future filled with hope and success, fear keeps you away from it.

Fear may have presided over me for a long time, but I wasn't going to let it lose to love. So I held on to the most precious Bible verse: "Love the Lord your God with all your heart and with all your soul and with all your mind and with all your strength" (Mark 12:30 NIV).

With this verse in mind, I continued to praise God, even when it hurt the most. God then became my friend, my confidant, and my only hope for the future. Bible verses then instilled positivity and guidance through what felt like the most confusing and challenging time of my life.

If I could offer any advice to anyone who is living in fear or is afraid of something, it would be to live your life in spite of the fear. Don't let it have control over your life. Don't allow fear to be the reason for something. Instead, let something be despite the fear of it. We all have something we are afraid of, whether we like to admit it or not, but if we let fear dictate our lives, we are only going to miss out on the life we are capable of. If you dread interviews, like most people do, it doesn't mean you are incapable or unskilled for the job, it only means you aren't good with interviews. But if getting the job means going through all those harrowing questions, do it anyway! So what if you're bad with interviews. So what if you lack the experience to start your own business. So what if you've never given a public speech before. You are not the only person who is afraid. People have overcome their fears and even turned them into success. There is a secret ingredient to overcoming fear. The solution is to do it anyway, and to do it being afraid. In other words, experience your fear.

What do I mean by this? I'll give you an example from my own life choices. I was terrified of going to the psychiatrist because of my fear attached to the stigma and misconceptions around mental health. I thought it was something I needed to get through on my own, but I desperately needed to get better.

When I started dating and seeing people, the effects of depression and anxiety on my mental health created a lot of problems for me. Whenever I had an episode of depression and anxiety, I tended to ruminate on thoughts, and these thoughts would blur reality. I would often get paranoid about my thoughts, and then I became physically and mentally exhausted by them. My reaction would be to panic. This affected me and my relationship with the other person. I quickly realized that my situation wasn't ideal and that I needed professional help.

I visited a few doctors before settling for someone I thought was good. I was terrified of confiding in my doctor because I was afraid of my diagnosis. I thought I was far from being able to be "fixed." Misconceptions about mental health had created so much fear in me that I thought I'd be better off without help. How wrong I was. I met the doctor and he advised me to come back if things become bad. I went home, prayed, and waited. Things did get bad.

I went back to the doctor and was put on medication. After a few trials and errors with my medications, my body soon reacted positively to the medicines. My mind started experiencing calm and quietness, and I no longer had problems with sleep.

Soon, things started feeling normal and I became more rational. I didn't hate going out and meeting with and talking to people. I wanted to go to work and church, and I even got into a relationship. These were some of the things I had always done, but never without mixed emotions. Before, I would rather have sulked at home while hating being at home, but now life felt normal. If only I had had the courage to treat my mental health with the proper care it deserved, I would have most likely been able to avoid so much heartache.

Life is difficult, but it only stays difficult if you allow it to be. Life becomes better when you make it better, and sometimes it requires you to break out of your comfort zone and go into unknown territory only to come across what you've been searching for.

Bible Verses to Remember

So do not fear, for I am with you; do not be dismayed,
for I am your God. I will strengthen you and help you;
I will uphold you with my righteous right hand.
Isa 41:10, NIV

Be strong and courageous. Do not be afraid;
do not be discouraged, for the LORD your
God will be with you wherever you go.
Josh 1:9, NIV

Even when I walk through the darkest valley, I
will not be afraid, for you are close beside me.
Ps 23:4, NLT

In the Midst of It All

*For I am the LORD your God who takes hold of your
right hand and says to you, Do not fear; I will help you.*
Isa 41:13, NIV

*The LORD is my light and my salvation—whom
shall I fear? The LORD is the stronghold of
my life—of whom shall I be afraid?*
Ps 27:1, NIV

*I prayed to the LORD, and he answered
me. He freed me from all my fears.*
Ps 34:4, NLT

Obedience

People who accept discipline are on the pathway to life,
but those who ignore correction will go astray

PROVERBS 10:17, NLT

PROVERBS IS A BOOK of wisdom! One can learn many things and grow by knowledge through it. When I was just a girl, my favorite books of the Bible were Proverbs and Psalms. I loved reading them because I wanted to be wise, joyful, and obedient. Proverbs says a person who accepts discipline or, in other words, is obedient to what is considered morally correct is already on the pathway to life, but someone who ignores it will only move away from the correct path.

We all enter this world without knowledge or wisdom. We grow and learn through listening and applying practically what is considered correct, lawful, and justified in our lives. The only way we can progress and move forward from our childish ignorance is through learning and accepting norms and teachings that mature us into grown adults. If we choose to ignore knowledge and wisdom, we are left with childish, foolish beliefs.

"The fear of the LORD is the beginning of knowledge, but fools despise wisdom and instruction" (Prov 1:7 NIV).

The same applies to our Christian lives. If we want to mature in God, we need to make an effort to know more about him, and one of the things Jesus teaches us is obedience. By definition, obedience is compliance with an order, request, or law, or submission to another's authority. What is obedience in a Christian context? If obedience is submission to authority, then biblically speaking, obedience is submission to God, his law and commandments, and his instructions.

To have faith in God means more than believing in him for our salvation. God expects a kind of faith where we live out our days on earth to fulfill his commandments and instructions every day and every moment of our lives. Even when we walk through the valley and our days feel heavy, we make a choice to hear, believe, trust, and surrender to God and his word when we show true biblical obedience.

Jesus promises blessings to those who hear the word of God and puts it into practice.

"Jesus replied, 'But even more blessed are all who hear the word of God and put it into practice'" (Luke 11:28 NLT).

Obeying God in small matters is the first step to inheriting God's blessings. In times of trouble, we often feel compelled to complain, frown, and even reject the truth of the Bible, but the Bible talks about God's grace for and presence with people who seek him and rely on him in distressing times.

"But the LORD watches over those who fear him, those who rely on his unfailing love" (Ps 33:18 NLT).

If you suffer from anxiety, you probably understand when I talk about the nonstop invasion of thoughts in my head. I used to think I had the most complicated relationship with my mind. I thought it didn't belong to me. Inside my head, my mind has thoughts my heart doesn't agree with. Should I trust my heart or believe the thoughts of my mind?

My thoughts are just mere thoughts. They lie to me, create false narratives, run rampant, and never cooperate. My heart, on the other hand, believes in things that are good for me. It hopes in things that matter, relies on the goodness of other people, and believes in things that are true and just. The case seems easy. I should choose my heart, but choosing my heart isn't always easy. Like many, my ego wants to dominate and rule my life. I think acting on my thoughts is right simply because of the justification that "what I think is right." This only paves the way to disobedience.

When God commands me to trust in him, instead I choose to trust in my mortal ways and thinking, which always seem to let me down time and again, only leading to more problems, heartaches, and letdowns. Emotions and thoughts blur the reality of what's in front of us, but God holds sovereignty over it. We need to stop worshiping the thoughts in our head. We need to stop giving them the attention they never should hold and give it back to the One who deserves it.

I once read that our mind is a false god, unworthy of our time and attention.[1] We are created by a God who understands his creations and has imparted knowledge and wisdom to mankind throughout the years so that we can learn to understand him and, in turn, understand our humanness. He sent his Son to give salvation and truth—all we need is to claim it.

We can't always prevent what information and thoughts go inside our minds, but we can choose which have governance over our lives, and we can choose how we react to them. Replace your negative thoughts with biblical truth. A biblical truth can be applied to any thought that comes your way. Take a Bible verse and its meaning and intention, and apply it to the thought in your head. For example:

Thought: "I need to have more control over my life so that I can cope better."

Bible verse: "Let the wicked man forsake his own way and the unrighteous man his own thoughts; let him return to the LORD, that He may have compassion, and to our God, for He will freely pardon. 'For My thoughts are not your thoughts, neither are your ways My ways,' declares the LORD. For as the heavens are higher than the earth, so My ways are higher than your ways and My thoughts than your thoughts'" (Isa 55:7–9 ESV).

How you can apply this Bible verse: You don't need to have control over every aspect of your life or your thoughts. Forsake (which means to leave behind) your thoughts because God has other thoughts for you. His thoughts are better than yours!

1. Stein, "Thoughts Are Just Thoughts."

Our willingness to hear the word of God and apply it to our lives may not always change our circumstances, but it can change our character and our closeness to God. We can't define or foretell the blessings that God has promised to each one of us, but we can trust they can come in ways and disguises that we least expect, and that they will be what we need the most.

Most times we can never understand why bad things happen, but they do. Your depression, anxiety, or any other mental illness may never be justified or can never be understood, but we can leave all that to God and accept in its place God's divine healing, peace, and purpose. We can surrender it to God to change a once-negative emotion and situation into something purposeful. Make a choice to obey God and do it with love, and watch him do wonderful works in your life!

Bible Verses to Remember

And this is love: that we walk in obedience to his commands.
2 John 1:6, NIV

"We must obey God rather than human beings!
Acts 5:29, NIV

But don't just listen to God's word. You must do what it says. Otherwise, you are only fooling yourselves.
Jas 1:22, NLT

Therefore everyone who hears these words of mine and puts them into practice is like a wise man who built his house on the rock.
Matt 7:24, NIV

Obedience is better than sacrifice, and submission is better than offering the fat of rams.
1 Sam 15:22, NLT

Truth

Jesus said, "If you hold to my teaching, you are really my disciples. Then you will know the truth, and the truth will set you free."

JOHN 8:31, NIV

WE'VE ALL BELIEVED A lie. Whether it was harmful to us or not, somewhere in our lives we've been coerced into believing something that wasn't true while thinking it was right the whole time.

Lies lead people to sin. Sin leads to fear. Fear leads to bondage. Bondage is Satan's hold on humans that prevents them from living the life God has for them. Most people think bondage is an addiction to a corrupting behavior. Believing things that are not true is the first step toward bondage.

In Nancy Leigh DeMoss's bestseller, *Lies Women Believe: And the Truth that Sets Them Free*, she examines lies and how we become deceived and led into bondage.

Satan plants a lie about us, about God, about sin, about people, and about almost anything. When we listen to a lie and dwell on it, we start believing it, and soon we start acting on it. When we believe a lie, we reject the truth and our lives begin on a foundation that separates us from God.

That's what happened in the Garden of Eden. The first sin committed against God was an act of disobedience that resulted from believing a lie. The same happened in the following generations. People from all walks of life have followed Eve and Adam's mistake. You and I are no different.

Lies can be of and about anything. You may have believed a lie about your life, your family, or your relationship, but the most destructive lies are those about God.

One day when I was around twenty-six years old, I randomly ran into a man who was much older than me. At that moment, all I could think of was this man being very uncomfortably familiar. He spoke to me and then left very soon afterward. Weeks later I went spiraling down, feeling depressed and ashamed, with unsettling and confusing memories of this particular man. I'm not sure why, but this random meeting had brought up repressed memories from my childhood.

These memories caused so much confusion and shame in me, and I didn't know how to handle it. It wasn't just what did and did not happen—I feared the chaos that was happening inside my head.

To put it plainly, the audio-visual device inside my head was turned up to its loudest and every time I thought of something else or wanted to quiet it down, the pressure would intensify, leaving scars and wounds on my thoughts and feelings and a perpetual feeling of fear and worry. I could never keep my eyes shut for more than five seconds before my brain would allow my thoughts to wander off to places, scenarios, and conversations that only left a mental and emotional disturbance. There were times I thought I was going crazy or was losing grip of my mind. Other times, I felt defeated.

One night, I lay in bed troubled and restless, and cried out to God. "Why? Why would you allow such a thing to happen? I have believed in you and trusted you, and now this happens."

I pondered what it would be like to have a different life. What would it be like if I had a healthy mind? A thought that said "I would be happier and more successful" crept into my mind.

What would life be like if my emotions were more stable? Another thought said, "I would definitely be loved,"

To make things even more difficult, fear slowly crept in like an unwanted guest—it intruded my safest of places. It made me question everything. Fear is an enemy. It steals your peace and leaves behind only fragments of your faith. Fear is a tactic skillfully mastered by someone who only wishes to deprive you of good and true things. Fear is ungodly.

"For God has not given us a spirit of fear and timidity, but of power, love, and self-discipline" (2 Tim 1:7 NLT).

That night, I felt things I'd never felt. Thought of things I never do. Suddenly, I had nothing to look forward to. I tried hard to reassure myself, but it only made me exhausted. I could feel my will to fight fast declining. That night I felt darkness, but God is faithful. I felt God reassuring me and reminding me of his promises and where I could find them, even though the darkness felt heavy in my heart. I felt alone—like I was fighting on my own. Many hard nights followed. I would sleep peacefully for two or three nights and then unexpectedly, no matter how much I tried, fear and despair would pull me down the rabbit hole. Every time I tried to get up and pull myself together, there was someone saying, "Did God really say . . . ?"

". . . that he is here for you?"

". . . that he cares for you?"

". . . that he loves you?"

". . . that he has a future for you?"

Satan is deceitful, and boy is he cunning. No matter what positive thoughts I tried to encourage myself with, he always had something to beat me down. Nights became harrowing. I dreaded them, but every morning when I got out of bed I felt a soft tug in my heart, a gentle reminder to not forget my Bible verses—a reminder that I wasn't alone and that even if I felt alone, there was something left for me, waiting for me to open it and yield to its power.

I only wish I could write a story with a quick, unexpected, and triumphant victory. It would sure make this book more exciting, but it would only be a lie. It was a long road to recovery, but at every turn and every stop God was there, and there was a chance to experience his presence in my life. This has given me the great privilege of helping others like me.

There are many verses that brought truth and light into my life, but there was one in particular that silenced fear and darkness:

"So do not fear, for I am with you; do not be dismayed, for I am your God. I will strengthen you and help you; I will uphold you with my righteous right hand" (Isa 41:10 NIV).

Whatever lie Satan brings to the table, God bears the truth. He is a God that doesn't change. Our lives may change—and with it our emotions, feelings, thoughts, and beliefs—but "God is not man, that he should lie, or a son of man, that he should change his mind" (Num 23:19 ESV).

Whatever God has promised us, he is able to do. Whatever he has spoken, he will fulfill. Whatever you're going through—depression, anxiety, or trauma—there is a biblical truth to every lie our frail mind may believe. When faced with thoughts that only bring uncertainty and unbelief, turn to the truth in the Bible.

God displays his faithfulness in different ways. A lot of people want to see God's glory work through instant miracles and recoveries, but I can confidently tell you that experiencing God in the most intimate, private times is the most fulfilling feeling you can ever ask for.

Bible Verses to Remember

I the LORD do not change.
Mal 3:6, NIV

The grass withers and the flowers fade, but
the word of our God stands forever.
Isa 40:8, NLT

Jesus Christ is the same yesterday and today and forever.
Heb 13:8, NIV

Your word, LORD, is eternal; it stands firm in the heavens.
Ps 119:89, NIV

For the LORD will not forsake his people;
he will not abandon his heritage.
Ps 94:14, ESV

Pain

"I will not cause pain without allowing some-
thing new to be born," says the Lord.

ISAIAH 66:9, NCV

WE ALL FEEL PAIN. We all go through personal suffering. Both are inevitable. How we deal with our suffering is up to us. Suffering cannot be measured. One's person suffering is not greater than an-other's. Maybe you put in three extra hours of work for a week or a month—that doesn't mean you're permitted to put down someone who worked fewer hours than you.

Learn to show compassion without measure. One of the best and purest pieces of advice I've even been given about pain was by a psychiatrist I visited. He said, "Do not detach yourself from it [a traumatic experience], but don't give it any value. What happened in the past is not what makes you today."

What you need to keep in mind is that pain is temporary. Pain will make you feel lonely, isolated, and misunderstood.

Pain tested my faith. As days turned into months and months into years, my season of suffering dried up my faith. My hope di-minished. Too many times, I gave in to despair.

Everyone goes through trying times in their faith. The theo-logical phrase for it is "storms in life." This refers to challenges people go through in life: sickness, loss of loved ones, financial problems, trauma, and so on.

We've all felt pain. People mistreat us. Neglect us. Physically harm us. My pain made me long for clarity, normalcy, and freedom from depression and anxiety. It made me paranoid about love, sex, and relationships. I distanced myself from getting emotionally involved. I was never in any meaningful relationship.

My most difficult struggle was with unwanted thoughts and sleep paralysis. I lost count of the traumatic nights. I went days and weeks without sleep, and this continued in cycles for years.

I remember desperately looking for a way out. I went to counseling, both medical and spiritual. I threw myself into work. But the one thing that gave me hope was 1 Pet 5:10: "And after you have suffered a little while, the God of all grace, who has called you to his eternal glory in Christ, will himself restore, confirm, strengthen, and establish you" (ESV).

I waited and held on, and then the sleep paralysis stopped. The anxiety became reduced. Nights became manageable. And I started longing for a relationship and intimacy.

I can't recall when and I can't describe it in detail, but my traumatic experiences turned into passion. I started writing down my feelings and thoughts. It looked messy, contradicting, and amateurish but that is who I am.

I am convinced my suffering would have been worse and more prolonged if it wasn't for the comfort of the Scriptures. God cares about our pain, our hurt, and our mistakes, no matter how hurtful, ugly, or irreparable it may feel to us. God can heal it all.

A few of the most common questions asked when going through pain are "Why is there pain in life?" and "Why would God allow such pain?" It is understandable to question our purpose on earth if we go through something so hurtful. I only hope there's a way we can all avoid pain, but since pain is inevitable, we can see it in a different light. Pain doesn't have to cost you. Pain can be for a purpose. Whether physical, emotional, spiritual, or mental, pain can be managed by seeing the purpose in it. We can cope with pain far better when we focus on the positive outcome it can give us.

Pain

"For I consider that the sufferings of this present time are not worth comparing with the glory that is to be revealed to us" (Rom 8:18 NIV).

God uses pain to fulfill our life's purpose. He did it with Jesus and he can do with you and me. We can learn from loss, grief, and adversity by growing and improving ourselves.

"Even though Jesus was God's Son, he learned obedience from the things he suffered" (Heb 5:8 NLT).

We can use our pain for our own good and for the good of others. Pain can result in a positive transformation in our lives and in our relationships. When we confide in people, it brings us closer to them. Pain can help build relationships when we allow it to draw us closer to others instead of allowing it to tear down relationships.

Oftentimes when we go through pain, it makes us feel isolated and alone. We feel like no one can truly feel what we are going through. Although it may be true, in the same way that you can empathize with someone's grief and loss, others can empathize with you. Another way of using your pain for a purpose is by helping others in similar situations. You might not know the right words to say or how to help them in the right way, but you can offer support. Your pain is not greater or more significant than that of others. Pain can result in a mutual understanding. Allow pain to deepen and mature your relationships with others.

Pain can be a stimulus for self-growth. Going through life with personal suffering can expose your emotions and lead to situations you may never have felt and encountered if it wasn't for the pain. Pain forces you to find your inner strength and character to push through the storm. Human beings are wired to adapt to, survive, and evolve through their experiences. Pain can turn you into a better version of yourself. The choices you make on your life's path regarding pain can make you self-aware, resilient, sensitive, and self-reliant.

"More than that, we rejoice in our sufferings, knowing that suffering produces endurance, and endurance produces character, and character produces hope, and hope does not put us to shame" (Rom 5:3–5 RSV).

Finally, pain allows us to draw closer to God. He can be our source of comfort and assurance in healing from pain. When going through pain that hurts us physically and emotionally, our first instinct is to confide in a higher being. We cry out to God. Let your pain be heard through prayers. Use your prayers to express your emotions and feelings, no matter how dark and gray they might feel. Surrender to God in your most fragile state of suffering.

"The Lord is close to the brokenhearted and saves those who are crushed in spirit" (Ps 34:18 NIV).

Bible Verses to Remember

Come to me, all you who are weary and
burdened, and I will give you rest.
Matt 11:28, NIV

And the God of all grace, who called you to
his eternal glory in Christ, after you have suf-
fered a little while, will himself restore you
and make you strong, firm and steadfast.
1 Pet 5:10, NIV

Out of my distress I called on the Lord; the
Lord answered me and set me free.
Ps 118:5, ESV

Physical Appearance

Charm is deceptive and beauty is fleeting but a
woman who fears the Lord is to be praised.

PROVERBS 31:30, NIV

PHYSICAL APPEARANCE HAS BECOME a thing of obsession these days. We all want to look and feel good, but what happens when the need to look and feel good doesn't end?

It is normal for people to check their appearance. They look in the mirror, inspect their clothes, cover a physical flaw, and build the body they want. Adolescents, whose bodies change drastically, form a bad habit of incessantly worrying about their physical appearance. It is normal for teenagers to feel self-conscious, especially about bodily changes caused by puberty. They may feel embarrassed about the hair on their legs or be concerned about the shape or size of their breasts.

Body image issues aren't just a problem for adolescents. In a society where unrealistic body ideals are promoted and celebrated, people get caught up in harmful and negative body comparisons. As a result, many people feel anxious, sad, and ashamed, and have self-loathing. Unrealistic body standards affect people of different ages, both male and female.

Some men and women focus to an extreme on how they look and the ideal body weight. They get stressed and anxious about their appearance and what people think of them. They spend excessive amounts of time and money on makeup and styling. They constantly seek approval and assurances from others. Some individuals avoid social situations and romantic relationships because of their notions about their appearance.

A very common habit that raises your level of anxiety is anxious and negative self-talk. Edmund Bourne describes anxious self-talk as what you say to yourself in your own mind. It is the internal monologue that you engage in much of the time, although it may be so automatic and subtle that you don't notice it unless you step back and pay attention.[1] This kind of talk can play in your mind, which only makes matters worse. "What if people look at the way I dress and look?" "What if it makes me anxious?" This type of self-talk anticipates the worst before it even happens.

Another form of self-talk is negative self-talk: "I am not worthy." "Why was I even born?" Negative or self-critical thinking is a habit you need to let go of. Much of the anxiety created is born from negative thinking.

What is the most destructive kind of behavior that raises social anxiety, especially among women? Comparison: the thief of joy. Women tend to harm and wound their self-confidence by comparing themselves to others. Not only does comparison add to stress and anxiety and deprive you of your happiness and joy—it also degrades your identity. The reason why you don't look like someone else is because you're genetically made and spiritually commanded to look just the way you do. We are supposed to look different. Our differences are what make us special and unique, not weird and outcast.

Insecurities and negative thinking can rob you from experiencing the simple pleasures of life. Having a healthy body image means learning to embrace your imperfections and appreciating your unique beauty.

"I praise you, for I am fearfully and wonderfully made. Wonderful are your works; my soul knows it very well" (Ps 139:14 NIV).

---

1. Bourne, *Anxiety and Phobia Workbook*, 60.

Physical Appearance

We are created in the image of God. You are not only unique, special, and one of a kind but also a reflection of God. Every part of our body is heavenly inherited. Isn't it a joy and pride to look just the way we do? Why conform to the world's standard of beauty when you can look uniquely you? You can place your worth in things manufactured, or you can place it on your Creator and heavenly Father.

We are all made different and have our own personality traits, genetic inheritance, skills, talents, voices, and destiny. Don't spend your life comparing yourself with others and defining yourself by who you are not. Instead, look to God and discover all that he has created you to be in him.

Bible Verses to Remember

For you created my inmost being; you knit
me together in my mother's womb.
Ps 139:13, NIV

She is clothed with strength and dignity, and
she laughs without fear of the future.
Prov 31:25, NLT

You should clothe yourselves instead with the beauty
that comes from within, the unfading beauty of a
gentle and quiet spirit, which is so precious to God.
1 Pet 3:4, NLT

Forgiveness

Be kind and compassionate to one another, forgiving each other, just as in Christ God forgave you.

EPHESIANS 4:32, NIV

THE WORST THING ANYONE has ever said to me about forgiveness is this: "You need to forgive and move on. It could have been worse!"

The most difficult thing to do is to freely forgive someone who has hurt you. Things people do or say can hurt us. People who are hurt, hurt others. It can be betrayal in a relationship, physical or emotional abuse, or abandonment by family and friends, but most times, it is just spiteful words and actions from someone we care about.

Emotional hurt can have a significant impact on people. It may be trivial or serious and it can cause short-term or long-term effects, but one thing is sure: forgiveness without bitterness doesn't come naturally. It requires great maturity and understanding.

To let go of words and actions that have caused pain takes time. It requires intervention, healing, and reciprocation from the other person. Sometimes it takes more than effort. Sometimes it takes longer than expected.

Like all forms of healing, forgiveness is a process. It looks different for everyone, and people handle it very differently. There is no step-by-step guide on how to truly let go and forgive.

Forgiveness starts and ends with a choice—a choice to set yourself and others free.

When I was younger, my understanding of forgiveness was constricted by my level of emotional maturity. My perspective on forgiveness was selfish. I wanted to forgive because I needed people in my life. Once I was able to let go without fault-finding and self-justification, I found myself truly understanding what forgiveness meant.

"Get rid of all bitterness, rage and anger, brawling and slander, along with every form of malice. Be kind and compassionate to one another, forgiving each other, just as in Christ God forgave you" (Eph 4: 31–32 NIV).

I harbored a lot of bitterness, especially toward those closest to me. I had no reason to have such feelings toward them, but there I was, getting angrier and more bitter at every encounter. I kept my composure most of the time and reasoned with myself, which helped cool the tension and friction within those relationships, but then I would find myself back at the old, bitter place.

I was angry about my unexplained anxiety. I was lonely because of my episodes of paranoia and sleeplessness. I was confused by my past memories. I lost count of my sleep-paralysis attacks. My mental state was going against me. It took a toll on my physical health. Never was I at a healthy, normal weight.

Where could I start with forgiveness?

It's easier said than done to forgive and forget. For me, forgetting did more harm. How could I move on by letting it slide by as if nothing had happened? As if I never had to deal with an emotional toil? Why did Jesus teach us to offer forgiveness seventy times seven times (Matt 18:22)? Why did God hold us to such a high standard? If God expects us to forgive seventy times seven times, could it also mean that someone is allowed to cause hurt to others seventy times seven times as well?

This made me angry. How is that fair?

Why would a loving and just God deem this commandment acceptable?

Can someone justify hurting someone continuously and be forgiven at the very last minute?

Something wasn't right. The Scriptures had gotten it wrong—so I thought. But Jesus wasn't justifying sin; he was insisting on the importance of forgiveness: "For if you forgive other people when they sin against you, your heavenly Father will also forgive you. But if you do not forgive others their sins, your Father will not forgive your sins" (Matt 6:14–15 NIV).

Forgive and you will be forgiven. Forgiveness doesn't mean that the people who hurt us are freed from the consequences of their sin. It means we are freed from holding others to their wrongdoing. We are freed from seeking revenge, for it is up to God, who judges justly, to punish the sins and wrongdoings of the world.

"When they hurled their insults at him, he did not retaliate; when he suffered, he made no threats. Instead, he entrusted himself to him who judges justly" (1 Pet 2:23 NIV).

It isn't up to us how and in what nature the other person is held accountable for their wrongdoing—the same way it isn't up to the other person how and in what nature we extend forgiveness for their actions.

There are no specific instructions on how and when a person extends and receives forgiveness. There is no formal guide on how long it should take for you to forgive completely, or how you should let people know they are forgiven. It simply requires that you forgive in your heart and conscience and live in peace with the other person.

"Make every effort to live in peace with everyone and to be holy" (Heb 12:14 NIV).

Once you truly forgive someone, you experience peace. And as for people who have caused hurt and pain, forgiveness is gained through repentance.

People who have caused physical or emotional harm to someone else may experience guilt. Guilt is a core emotion that controls the social behavior of a person. Guilt is felt when someone is aware of or takes responsibility for a harmful, negative action inflicted on themselves or other people. There are many things that make a person feel guilty; these can range from something as harmless as feeling guilty for eating an extra slice of pizza to something more harmful, like hurting or abusing another person. Guilt is more than feeling upset with yourself. It combines feelings of distress, shame, anxiety, and regret.

Guilt can take an emotional toll on someone when unresolved. When someone is completely aware of their negative actions or spiteful words to someone else, it can leave trails of emotions that can harm a person's mental state and social behavior. Guilty feelings can make it difficult for someone to concentrate and think straight, and when left unresolved, guilt can lead to long-term effects like unwarranted emotional outbursts. Guilt can hold back a person from experiencing joy in life. It might even lead to mild or moderate depression. Guilty behaviors include avoiding social events, like parties, hesitation about celebrating your own birthday, moping around during vacations, self-loathing, and avoiding the person you have wronged.

If guilt is eating you inside out, let's take a look at the biblical perspective of forgiveness through repentance.

The concept of repentance in the Bible is "to change one's mind" in respect to one's behavior. Repentance does not only mean that you try to change or reverse a situation but also involves a change in the way we think intellectually and spiritually. It involves a deep sense of regret and sorrow toward past (negative) behavior and a need for genuine and sincere change in our character, beliefs, and thoughts—in other words, a conversion of the heart, soul, and mind.

In the Old Testament, there were expected rituals for repentance, but Jesus changed it all. We are all expected to repent spiritually, emotionally, and mentally before God through confession and a practical change in our lives. Genuine need for change involves recognition of the absolute need of the mercy of God in our frail human lives. It requires us to confess our sins before him and ask him to cleanse us from all unrighteousness.

"If we confess our sins, he is faithful and just and will forgive us our sins and purify us from all unrighteousness" (1 John 1:9 NIV).

God is one for forgiveness. The Bible says he is a God who is compassionate and merciful, slow to get angry and filled with unfailing love. He is not a God who remains angry forever and punishes us harshly, as we deserve. Instead, his unfailing love for those who fear him and call upon him is immeasurable, as far as the heavens from the earth. There is nothing you can do to change his mind about forgiveness. Seek God wholeheartedly, and may his mercy be upon you!

"He has removed our sins as far from us as the east is from the west" (Ps 103: 12 NLT).

Bible Verses to Remember

If my people, who are called by my name, will humble themselves and pray and seek my face and turn from their wicked ways, then I will hear from heaven, and I will forgive their sin and will heal their land.
2 Chr 7:14, NIV

If your brother or sister sins against you, rebuke them; and if they repent, forgive them.
Luke 17:3, NIV

Therefore there is now no condemnation for those who are in Christ Jesus.
Rom 8:1, NIV

Godly sorrow brings repentance that leads to salvation and leaves no regret, but worldly sorrow brings death.
2 Cor 7:10, NIV

Blessed is the one whose transgressions are forgiven, whose sins are covered.
Ps 32:1, NIV

Healing

Heal me, O Lord, and I will be healed

JEREMIAH 17:14, NIV

I WAS THIRTY YEARS old when I decided to seek medical help for my mental health. At that point, I wasn't sure what was happening to me, but I knew it wasn't normal for my mind to be in such a state. It was never at rest. At times, it left me feeling mentally and physically exhausted. I became delusional, and on some days I was convinced I was slowly losing my sanity.

Things became worse when I started losing sleep continuously, and the stress from working and living in a city I wasn't happy in accelerated things from bad to worse. On most nights, I would lie awake for hours, and my mind would drift off to endless thoughts of conversations, scenarios, what ifs, and what coulds. It was torturous. Not only did it bring up negative and anxious thoughts, but it also left me exhausted and delusional. The average amount of sleep I'd get was three hours a night, and after a few days of this, I would be so physically and mentally exhausted that my mind and body would just shut off, and these were the only times I'd get a whole night of sleep.

The nights I couldn't sleep, I would toss and turn, feeling frustrated and hating myself and my situation. I became resentful. My mental state prompted a sudden decision to quit my job and move back home. I had no plans and expectations from my sudden decision; I only had one thing on my mind—I could not let depression and anxiety rule my choices and decisions anymore. Whatever might happen, I had one clear motive: I needed to get better. I decided to trust God faithfully and blindly.

When I moved back home to Shillong, a place known for its slow, calm, relaxed living, I instantly felt better, but not healed. I tried my best to make changes to my routine just so my mind could savor some peace. I took a year-long break from working, dedicating myself to eating better and healthier, reading books, and writing more. I even decided to give dating a priority. I met people and went out on dates, but then I became so consumed with my own thoughts that I started believing them. These thoughts conflicted with my beliefs and behavior, and I was afraid for myself. I had never wanted things to change so badly. I was so afraid of the conflict in my head and in my heart, I was prepared to do anything to make things better.

I decided to consult a psychiatrist, and a few consultations later, I was put on medication for depression and anxiety. The medicines helped a great deal, and I was getting and feeling better by the day. Things were slowly getting back to normal. My mind was calm, my emotions were stable, I had no problems getting up, and I even decided to start working again. I was also experiencing love for the first time in my life. It was a slow process, but I was finally getting there.

There was a point in my past when I accepted defeat. I gave in and told myself I had to be okay with the fact that I wasn't okay, but the truth was that I didn't have to live with defeat. I didn't have to live with a chaotic mind and a restless soul. I wanted to live the life God had planned for me.

Healing is very personal and sometimes confusing. In the midst of all of it, I found myself taking one giant leap forward and being completely lost in my unfamiliar, foreign location. I didn't know what I was feeling or what to expect. Many times, I would just savor the moments where I felt peace and stillness. Some days,

I would look back at where I had been a year or two before. It was difficult not to get lost in my own thoughts.

There were ups and downs in my recovery. I went through a long period of time during recovery where I never prayed a word. I felt like I ran out of words to say or I just couldn't find anything to say. I stopped listening to gospel music, which I love, and instead would write more than usual, but I felt peace I hadn't felt in a very long time. This made me think and question myself a lot. "Am I really healing, or just going through another phase of my life?"

It felt strange to have my mind experience calm for a long stretch of time. Of course, it was partly because of the medications. The calm and quietness made me think, "Is this what normalcy feels like?"

I still have difficult days, but it has become more manageable. On nights when I lose sleep, I become discouraged and feel restless the following day. The same depressing thoughts invade and intrude on my peace. I remind myself not to allow my thoughts and emotions to fall back into the same old pattern of destruction. I put an effort into not allowing myself to wallow in my anxiety. I create new habits. Instead of sleeping in and doing nothing for days, I read an engaging book, do some chores, and keep myself away from isolation. I remind myself that God is always near, even when anxiety and depression make it feel like I am all alone.

What I've learnt so far is that recovery doesn't mean you are never going to feel depressed or anxious ever again. It means that when I have my bad days, things don't need to go from bad to worse. It gets better by the minute, by the hour, and by the day. I can go to bed thinking, "Today was one of those days. Tomorrow I can get up and start a new day."

Depression doesn't have to keep me isolated and alone or sad and feeling low. Depression is just a temporary state that I can always get through. My thoughts and feelings are not my master. My reality is what governs me, and the reality is that God has given me a life I can live—and live well. Challenges and trials only reveal to me my human nature. My flesh is weak, but my spirit is made fresh and new by the Spirit of God that dwells inside of me. He is bigger than my depression and my anxiety.

Jesus is my priority. He is my salvation and my reason for living. This life is only temporary. I can have moments of joy, happiness, and beauty all around, and sometimes moments of pain. My soul may long for heaven on earth—a place where there is no pain, no hardship, and no sorrow. When my time on earth has come to an end, I want to know that I've lived the best I could have. I've known God in my heart, and one day my spirit will meet him. Till then, I want to live on earth dutifully and faithfully.

I never felt the need to know exactly what caused me so much distress and why, or what recovery is supposed to feel like. All I could think of was 1 Pet 5:10: "And after you have suffered a little while, the God of all grace, who has called you to his eternal glory in Christ, will himself restore, confirm, strengthen, and establish you" (NLT).

In the same way I trusted the word of God during my trials, I decided to entrust the very same word with my recovery. I may never know what tomorrow will bring, but my God does, and there's no greater peace than the knowledge that I have nothing to lose in trusting God.

My hope for anyone reading this is that whatever you are going through or have gone through, you may find the peace and comfort you desire in the faithful words of God. I pray that his words will abide in you and you in him, now and forever.

Bible Verses to Remember

I have heard your prayer and seen
your tears; I will heal you.
2 Kgs 20:5, NIV

Do not let your hearts be troubled and do not be afraid.
John 14:27, NIV

Healing

Come to me, all you who are weary and
burdened, and I will give you rest.
Matt 11:28, NIV

He gives strength to the weary and in-
creases the power of the weak.
Isa 40:29, NIV

Then they cried to the LORD in their trouble,
and he saved them from their distress.
Ps 107:19, NIV

"Nevertheless, I will bring health and heal-
ing to it; I will heal my people and will let
them enjoy abundant peace and security."
Jer 33:6, NIV

Part 3

Asking for Help

The way of a fool is right in his own eyes,
but a wise man listens to advice.

PROVERBS 12:15, ESV

I WAS ASHAMED ABOUT my mental state. Even before the doctor confirmed it was depression, I was ashamed. I was afraid. I was afraid of losing control over my life and over my own mind. I didn't want to give the reigns of control to medications, therapy, and counseling, or so I thought. I was uneducated, mostly because of the misconceptions I myself believed and society had me believe. I didn't want to lose myself. I wanted to hold on to what I believed, and the belief was that I could get through it all on my own. All I needed was support, understanding, and a miracle. I didn't know what I expected from God and from my family and friends. It felt like I'd done so much for myself and failed miserably. If people could show me kindness and compassion, then maybe I'd be braver. If only God fulfilled the desires of my heart, then maybe it wouldn't hurt so bad.

Many times I wondered what would have happened if only I'd asked for help sooner or had been more vocal and shared more.

If I'd have let people know how I was feeling, things wouldn't have been so bad. I can't tell you the number of times my friends told me to get help and I chose to ignore their advice, not because I thought they were wrong but because I was afraid. I was afraid of my diagnosis. I was terrified. I thought it would change me and my life, and I didn't want that to happen. I wanted things to stay the same, but I also knew I should feel better. Whatever that meant.

All my life I thought, "My life is easy. I have nothing to complain or frown or make a scene about. I had support and love from parents, closeness and friendship with my cousins, sisterhood from friends, and open opportunities for the future. Where could I start if none of those things were good enough for me or good enough for my mental health. I thought people with a good, normal life shouldn't have problems with their mental health. Mental-health issues are reserved for people with childhood trauma, abuse, and abandonment. Financial loss, cheating spouses, miscarriages. Grief, heartbreak, pressure. These were the grounds for mental illness. And if I didn't have any of these, why should I have a problem?

I was young, naïve, and misunderstood—not by other people but by myself. I didn't understand what depression can make you feel. I didn't know what anxiety can do. But I do blame other people too. I've heard people say that Christians should never feel depressed because we have Jesus. Depression is for those who have lost hope in God. It doesn't happen to you and me. And I believed them.

I want people to know that embracing the fact that I live with depression has been the best thing I've done for myself. It made me true, it made me brave, and it made me hopeful. I've never felt more loved now than before. I am not less because of my depression, neither am I more. I am myself. I am forgiven, I am saved, and I am accepted. I am what God made me.

I don't know why I was conditioned to think that if we were saved, we ought to be and feel perfect in every way. I didn't see the truth: We are saved from our sins. I need God more than ever because I am a human, sinful in nature, imperfect in every way— and these flaws need a perfect God. These loveless parts need a pure, loving God. This chaotic mind and restless soul need a savior. And I have him.

One of the ways seeking help has helped me is by enabling me to see reality for what it is. Depression can blur reality. It makes everything around you less valuable. Speaking from personal experience, depression makes you find security in the invaluable, like you have to settle for less simply because that's just how it is. There's nothing you can do and there's nothing you can change.

Everything about that is wrong. The truth is that you can change. Things can get better. You can't make the gray skies go away, but you can enjoy the clear blue skies. And if you put an optimistic mind to it, the gray skies are not too bad either. It's not bad when you have someone to snuggle with, or a good book to read, or an umbrella to go out with, or some good, hot coffee.

One of the things I'm leaving behind is the desperate need to feel okay or to feel better. I hope you understand that for people with chronic illness, this need turns into desperation, but for others it is simply out of a human need for more. People always want to feel happier than before, more loved than they do, and more successful than others thought—more and more. I don't have to have happy days every day. I don't have the need to be okay and perfect all the time. It's fine if I fall short in all those things. It's normal if I'm sad or if I lose sleep, and it's normal to ask for help.

One of the things that helped me find acceptance in who I am and what I'm going through is emotional maturity. I no longer have trouble seeing the imperfections and flaws in my life. I understand that I am only human and that my human body is susceptible to illness in the same way it is susceptible to growth and change. I recognized that my younger self didn't understand much; I lacked knowledge, the confidence, and even the courage. I feel different these days. The years have changed me. They have evolved me, and I don't intend on staying the same. Change is good. It has for been for me. I want to change. My mother once taught me that the fruits of the Spirit are called fruits because we can see them, eat them, and be nourished by them. They aren't hidden inside the tree and in its branches and roots. They are there for all to see.

"But the fruit of the Spirit is love, joy, peace, forbearance, kindness, goodness, faithfulness, gentleness and self-control" (Gal 5:22–23 NIV).

I don't want people to see the depression in me and what it is capable of doing to my body and my mind. I want them to see love, joy, peace, forbearance, kindness, goodness, faithfulness, gentleness, and self-control. I want these to have mastery over my life.

If you're showing signs and symptoms of a mental condition, don't be afraid to ask for help. The sooner you reach out, the faster you will recover. It's normal for someone to feel sad, frustrated, and anxious at times, but it's important to be able to recognize when a mood or behavioral change has become more than just a temporary thing. When you see the signs, try to make changes in your life by starting with small steps. Don't let depression or anxiety get in the way of your life. Instead, adopt healthy habits like regular sleep habits, nutritious meals, and a healthy amount of physical activity. If signs and symptoms of a mental condition are becoming persistent, last longer, and affect your daily life in a negative way, it is better you seek professional help. You may need medications to help manage it.

I had a bad habit of googling for answers. Please avoid this. You won't find answers on the internet. Depression can manifest itself in many ways. What you're going through may be very personal and different from what other people experience. The best way is to talk to a professional and follow his or her advice.

There are a lot of misconceptions about mental health that contribute to the stigma surrounding it. This can discourage people from seeking help and talking about it freely. Mental health problems are common. Millions of people around the world experience all sorts of problems related to their mental health. Statistically, depression is said to be the most common mental health problem. Nowadays, especially in more developed countries, mental health has been given the attention it deserves. One of the most damaging misconceptions is that mental illness is only a result of emotional or spiritual weakness. Mental illness is no different from a physical illness. A physical illness affects the body more than the mind, and a mental illness affects the mind more than the body. Another misconception is that people with mental illness become dependent on medication and therapy. Again, medications for mental illness are prescribed in the same way as medications for a physical illness. Dependency starts when someone abuses the medications. This can happen with anyone, not just people with mental problems. Therapy is for when you need someone's professional help and confidential advice that you cannot get from untrained confidants. One of the saddest misconceptions is one about suicidal thoughts. Suicidal thoughts are often symptoms of depression or a related mood disorder. Suicidal feelings can go away. They are not permanent thoughts and feelings that need to be acted on. Once you begin to receive proper care for the cause of your suicidal thoughts, they will diminish and you will feel better.

If you're afraid to reach out, I advise you to talk with someone close to you. Someone you feel safe with. They may know others who are also struggling and can offer you advice. In the next chapter, I talk about certain coping methods for depression and anxiety. You can read more on how certain lifestyle changes can bring about positive changes in your mental health.

Part 4

Coping with Depression & Anxiety

Do you not know that your bodies are temples of the Holy
Spirit, who is in you, whom you have received from God

1 CORINTHIANS 6:19, NIV

A HEALTHY LIFESTYLE ISN'T just practical, it is also spiritual and
biblical. You cannot expect a peaceful mind amidst a chaotic lifestyle. A stress free life only exists in 'imagination land'. Here, we
are free from worrying, free from being under pressure, free from
facing uncertainty, free from debts and responsibilities and free
from a mundane life. We all wish we can avoid stress but a stress
free life is something almost unachievable and unnatural.

No one wants to sit all day with absolutely nothing to do just
to avoid stress. We all want to be productive. A healthy lifestyle
starts with being productive in a way that is just enough and just
as pleasant. We want to end each day with small victories of our
own. Now that is something hard to come by. Living a life that is
productive and fulfilling comes with practice. A healthy lifestyle
takes practice and commitment.

As we all know by now, stress can trigger a slew of health and
mental problems but there is hope. There are many ways we can

reduce and manage stress and not let it get in the way of our daily lives. A healthy lifestyle is taking care of your physical, emotional, spiritual and mental wellbeing. It starts with adopting practices that are good for you and letting go of bad habits that may add to your stress levels.

A healthy way of coping with a mental illness is treating it no different from a physical illness. It is not your fault if you are struggling with a mental condition. Regardless, of how it feels, a mental sickness is a result of the fall. God doesn't make mistakes. We are not a mistake or an accident. Our flesh can be flawed. Our mind may betray us. Our emotions can be reckless but God is constant and never changing. With Him there is healing, redemption and forgiveness.

The first step to recovery is recognizing you have a problem and giving it the same attention you would if you had a physical illness. Know the signs and symptoms of depression and anxiety and consult with a doctor. Not all symptoms are present in a person, if you are unaware or confused with your symptoms, don't be alarmed. Confide in someone close, or better yet, visit a psychiatrist and seek their professional advice. With the right treatment, depression and anxiety becomes manageable and recoverable. If you have suicidal thoughts or suicidal ideation, seek medical help right away.

Be honest and open with your doctor about your symptoms or simply confide in them about how you feel and what you've been thinking lately. It is important that you keep up with your medication regimen when prescribed by your doctor.

Mental illness is real and common. It is treatable and people with it can get better. Don't hesitate to seek help for yourself or for a loved one.

Things You Can Do for
Your Mental Health

Get Proper Sleep

TOO MUCH SLEEP CAN make you lazy and too little sleep can exhaust you. Sleep is one of the most important factors in a healthy lifestyle. Getting enough quality sleep at the right time helps stabilize your physical and mental health. Anxiety, depression, and any mental or physical illness can seriously affect your sleep patterns and make existing problems worse.

Inadequate sleep causes more problems than just exhaustion and tiredness. It can make it difficult for you to concentrate during the day. Getting adequate sleep is vital to stabilizing your mood, energy, and chemical balance in your brain. Here are simple tips that can help you get a good night's sleep during times when it is difficult:

- Get some light physical activity during the day.

- Focus on getting restful sleep rather than getting enough sleep.

- Avoid napping during the day.

- Avoid caffeine, alcohol, and nicotine and focus on healthy foods.

- Try to wake up and go to bed at the same time every day.

- Read a book, listen to music, or meditate, if it helps.

- If required, consult a doctor for medications to help you sleep better.

Physical Activity Is Important

Physical activities improve mental health. A physical activity doesn't have to be just strenuous exercise. It can involve any type of activity that makes you active, like walking, biking, hiking, running, brisk walking, and engaging in hobbies and sports.

It's important to note that when your body is stressed and exhausted from lack of sleep, it's advisable to get a light form of exercise rather than a whole-body workout. Anxiety can make it difficult and uncomfortable for some people to get out of bed and out the door, but you need the physical exercise. Motivate yourself and get some much-needed physical therapy. Here are some health benefits from regular physical activities:

- Improved sleep
- Stress relief
- Improved mood
- Increase in energy and stamina
- Reduced cholesterol and improved cardiovascular fitness

Maintain a Healthy Work-Life Balance

Exhausting yourself from work doesn't benefit you at all. Balancing your professional and personal lives can be challenging, but it is essential. A good work-life balance has positive effects; it can reduce stress, lower the risk of burnout, and give a sense of well-being. It is a priority to regularly keep a balance between your personal and professional lives. Make sure you have quality time for your family and friends and personal interests.

One of the best methods to achieve a balanced life is prioritizing your time. Have set work hours for yourself and stick to them.

You don't need to burn the midnight oil for presentations, reports, sales, bonuses, and recognition every day. Don't overlook setting aside time for your personal relationships and "me time." Invest in others and yourself passionately, the way you do with your work. Find time to rest during the day, which may involve lying on the couch doing nothing, reading a book, listening to some soothing music, meditating, doing breathing techniques, and so on. You might want to involve yourself in some light recreational activity you find fun, calming, or therapeutic. Some examples are watching a movie, going to the gym, having a date night, painting, doing sports, walking, cooking, baking, and anything else you consider fun.

Get Rid of Those Old Habits

Anxiety isn't only caused by big, traumatic events in life. Mostly it's caused by the daily pressures in life that add stress and bring on unnecessary anxiety. Bad habits contribute to generalized anxiety. Getting rid of these old habits can bring healing and a renewed sense of self. Stop the negative self-talk, avoid junk and skipping meals, and stick to eating healthy. Don't overcompensate with caffeine, nicotine, and alcohol. Get off social media and make time for yourself and other people. Stop procrastinating and instead manage your time to your advantage. Don't deprive yourself of rest and sleep, and most importantly, don't beat yourself up. Mental health is worth fighting for.

Live Out Your Passion

We are not meant to wake up, work, and go to bed. Life is so much more than the fast-paced business world. We all have passions that ignite our soul. For some, their passion pays the bills, but if life has another purpose and other directions for you, you can still live to enjoy the small pleasures that your passion brings you.

Part of living a balanced life is having a steady job that brings you a steady income and also having a life outside your job. This involves living and pursuing activities that makes you generally happy and content. Your passion is your God-given talent, creativity, skill, and desire. Music, art, literature, charity, helping people, animals, faith, ministry and worship, hobbies and sports, traveling and adventure, leadership, service, teaching, learning, health and fitness, and relationships can be your individual passion. Figure out what you love and start living for it or with it.

Consult a Doctor

When I decided to finally seek medical help for my depression, I visited a few doctors and counselors before feeling confident with someone. After a few consultations, I was put on medication, which I had to take for almost a year. The medicines helped me tremendously. I was able to sleep and concentrate, which reduced my anxiety and other problems caused by sleepless nights. My emotions stabilized and I was able to think clearly. If your mental state is putting you in a place where daily life becomes difficult, I recommend seeking medical help. I was in denial for years, and I was always anxious about confiding in a psychiatrist. If you are reluctant to seek help, I personally advise you to take small steps to recovery. You can start by talking to a friend or family member about your mental health and slowly making your way to medical help, or vice versa.

Pray for Your Mental Health

Take control over your mental health through praying. The Bible encourages us to pray with thanksgiving. This means we should pray with a heart of thanksgiving even when it feels heavy and burdened. You may feel hopeless and lonely with uncontrolled emotions, but God doesn't judge us. He is near to those who are brokenhearted. Present your requests to God. Pray for healing for your mind and comfort for your soul. You can pray when you begin to seek medical or professional help. You can pray for understanding and support from your friends, family, and community. Pray for forgiveness of sin, for relief from guilt and shame, and most importantly, for God's will to be done in your life.

Conclusion

THE COOL SHILLONG WEATHER never fails to bring me rest. Whenever I feel depleted, I like to rest at home and look out to the clear blue skies with kisses of clouds and the tall pine trees nearby that always sway with the wind. I always think of God when I look at nature. There's so much beauty all around, and we fail to appreciate it. On such days, I find rest and peace in my writing. I never thought this chaotic mind would find so much harmony and tranquility in the simple art of expression. I've realized that my writing is nurtured through reading, another hobby that brings me comfort. I love to read a good book, especially one that is creatively written and adds to my imagination. I also like to read ones that add to my knowledge. Whenever I read, I imagine the reader being like me. She must have found inspiration from her own pain and hurt. I imagine her life being monotonous and raveling like mine. But her words are what bring so much empathy.

Today I'm reading a *New York Times* best seller and in the last chapter, the writer has a difficult time finding words to leave with her readers. How appropriate and what a relief! I've been struggling to find words of my own. What can I say to make this transformational to you? What piece of advice can I leave you with?

I have no more words but those I tell myself. The peace and comfort you're searching for can be found. If you allow yourself, you'll find that part of you that longs for God. It's untainted and unadulterated. It's something that you cannot buy or earn or work for. It's a piece of you that doesn't belong to a person. It's a piece designed for closeness and relationship with something more. More than the natural. Higher than earthly things.

We give so much of ourselves that at times we forget about what matters. We forget the good times, the special moments, the friends and family, and the praise and worship. We forget to just be human.

As I grow into the years, I want to learn to hold on to what matters and not allow myself to get lost in the material, the inauthentic, and the temporary. I want to take a step back if I have to and allow for something else or someone else to take its place next to me. I want to love, laugh, write, go on dates, and kiss. I want to feel connected, empowered, and purposeful. I want to do a lot of things without feeling required to. I want to live without the burden of the need to feel or be better.

And if my mind ever turns on me and does the things my mind sometimes does, I'll remember to be still and rest. To practice patience and survival. To cope with hope and thanksgiving. And I'll learn to react to all the things that used to send me into so much frenzy and anxiety with tenderness and care. That is new and foreign to me, but I'll learn along the way.

I don't know what would happen if I continued letting my thoughts and feelings have control over me. I don't know what that would look like a year or ten years from now. I imagine a very torn-down version of me, helpless and ashamed.

I once had a conversation with my girlfriends about how we had hoped our futures would look when we were younger. We'd all had similar hopes. We had all thought we'd be married by thirty with a fancy job. When I was younger, I thought getting married was something so natural that happens to everyone once they reach a particular age. Now I can only sigh for that young child.

So our future didn't really go the way we had hoped it would. And I have a feeling it never will. It'll never go as planned, and that's okay. I've stopped looking at life as a long list of things to do and accomplish and instead try to make the most of what's given to me.

Conclusion

Many people make the terrible mistake of building a life in their heads and a god of their own interpretations. But the truth is in the simplicity of what's already written.

Bibliography

Bourne, Edmund J. *The Anxiety and Phobia Workbook.* 7th ed. Oakland: New Harbinger, 2020.

DeMoss Wolgemuth, Nancy. *Lies Women Believe: And the Truth That Sets Them Free.* Chicago: Moody, 2018.

Liang, Roy. "The 8 Types of Love—According to the Ancient Greeks." *Roy Liang* (blog), May 23, 2020. https://allad201314.medium.com/the-8-types-of-love-accoding-to-the-ancient-greeks-97bff653bbfd.

McIntosh, Diane. *This Is Depression: A Comprehensive, Compassionate Guide for Anyone Who Wants to Understand Depression.* Vancouver: Page Two, 2019.

Sproul, R. C. *What Is Biblical Wisdom? (Crucial Questions).* Orlando: Reformation Trust, 2020.

Stein, Michael. "Thoughts Are Just Thoughts: How to Stop Worshiping Your Anxious Mind." Anxiety & Depression Association of America. https://adaa.org/learn-from-us/from-the-experts/blog-posts/consumer/thoughts-are-just-thoughts.

Wallace, Lawrence. *Cognitive Behavioral Therapy: 7 Ways to Freedom from Anxiety, Depression, and Intrusive Thoughts.* N.p.: Independent Publishers, 2016.